M000248085

SHOWERING WITH NANA

SHOWERING WITH NANA:

CONFESSIONS OF A SERIAL (~~KILLER~~) CAREGIVER

CATHY SIKORSKI

Published 2015 by HumorOutcasts Press
Printed in the United States of America

ISBN: 0-692-44041-0
EAN-13: 978-069244041-4

Cover art and design by Joe Hetro

For my Mom, Mary Ann,

My daughters, Rachel and Margot,

My grandmothers, sisters, nieces, aunts, girlfriends

and every woman who has cared for me…

And for my husband, John,

who has never wavered in his support

Acknowledgments

For more than 20 years, I have been toiling over this book with so much love and support that I cannot forego the opportunity to thank those who have led, pushed, coddled and cuddled me along the way.

I have had a few trusted friends like Terri Newmyer and Jean Dames who were kind enough and honest enough to read my drafts and offer clear and helpful advice.

Steve Parolini, the Novel Doctor, was a godsend who was able to give such great editorial advice, while still understanding the humor all along the way. He is a fine and exceptional editor, and I thank him for his generous guidance.

Donna Cavanagh of HumorOutcasts Press. Where would I be without Donna? She is the editor and publisher extraordinaire that we all dream of. She loves and 'gets' the humor of life and she trusted my vision. I am so happy that she is not just my editor and publisher, but now also my friend. Every once in a while someone special enters your life and you can't believe how lucky you are….that's my Donna Cavanagh.

I am so lucky to be married to John Sikorski who welcomed my Nana and all my crazy relatives into his unsuspecting life, always with love and kindness. He has always supported my career changes, choices and challenges. Every girl should be so fortunate.

My daughters, Sarah (who my sister let me 'claim' as my first daughter), Rachel and Margot have been the best cheerleaders a Mom could ever want. They have never doubted my talent, even when I did. They have grown to be amazing women and we are a blessed family indeed. I am grateful for their advice and their love every single day.

My Mom and I have become great friends. I am so thankful I had the chance to grow up and find the 'person' behind the Mom. She continues to this day to be my 'go-to' girl as my caregiving continues with others. And she is forever telling her children how proud she is of them.

If you are lucky enough to have sisters and girlfriends like Tina, Caren, Maggie, Heidi, Linda, Terri, Sally, Lisa, Joanne, Barb, Terri (another one), Tootie, Carol, Sandy, Wendy, Monica, Jean, Therese and Laura you have a life beyond wildest riches. And if I have forgotten to mention any one of my amazing women friends, and I'm sure I have been remiss, please forgive me as I truly love and appreciate each and every one of you.

In loving, loving and heartfelt memory of my sister, Cindy....a truly beautiful girl.

If you scored a 92 on a test, you'd be happy. If you live to 92, you'd be lucky. If you have to take care of someone who is 92, you'd be crazy.

When my father, an Army helicopter pilot, died in a crash in 1961, my mother co-opted Nana into being our second parent. There were five children and one on the way. To the best of my knowledge, my grandmother never complained once.

Nana was 65 years old at the time we relocated from Germany to Pennsylvania to live with her and Pop-Pop. We moved into her row home or half-a-double "temporarily" even though my mother owned her own home across town. It was supposed to be a temporary move.

But we never left.

Six children and four adults, including my great-grandmother, found themselves stuffed into a tiny three-bedroom, one-bathroom house shaped like a railroad car. And just like a railroad car, we had to shuffle sideways to get through traffic in the hallway.

Having raised four children of her own during the Depression, with no extra anything, Nana knew plenty about the simple labor of raising a family. Hers was a labor of love—and make no mistake about it—it was labor.

My mother and Nana have lived together since those first grief-filled days in the sixties. My mother's remarriage offered a brief respite to that living arrangement. Since I was a stay-at-home mom, on leave from my law practice, and my mother and stepfather spent their winters in Florida, I was nominated to take care of Nana. Nana was not allowed to stay home alone. She had recently begun to develop some ideas and habits that made it unsafe for her to be without some kind of supervision. Nana had started to forget things such as leaving pots on the stove or going outside and puzzling over the reason why. She still thought of

- 1 -

herself as independent and capable, and she did make a meal for herself once in a while. I mean if coffee...and coffee...and coffee...can be considered a meal.

None of this should have been a surprise. After all, isn't forgetfulness kind of expected when you reach 92? But still, this presented us with a problem. None of us would even consider the "N" word—no, not that one—I mean nursing home. So I was chosen to offer guidance and protection as needed.

It didn't take long for me to discover just how needed those two things were.

WEEK ONE AND WEEK TWO

The first week of her stay was fairly effortless. Nana wasn't causing much damage. In the morning, she would eat her toast with jelly, walk up and down the long driveway with the dog, Troon, and then take a nap. Conveniently, her nap schedule lined up perfectly with that of my two-year-old, Rachel. I was truly blessed. This routine, with an occasional lunch date, a trip to the grocery store, and a few errands thrown in, was proving to be a piece of cake. Managing Nana would not be difficult at all.

I have never been anything but comfortable with Nana. She's been a complete bubble of comfort for all my brothers and sisters too. And I'm fairly certain she did the same for my mom since we ended up all squinched together in that old 1920's house. We were always just one big bubble of comfort...until the day things started to change.

To put a positive spin on it: Nana in some ways began to act like her old self. She had always been a domestic dynamo just like my mother. But when you put 'dynamo' and a 92-year-old woman in the proverbial blender, you don't end up with a smoothie. What you get is a whirlwind of cleaning, cooking, child care and general 1940's housewifery.

In week two, Nana decided she would help with the house cleaning. My grandmother was always an expert at cleaning. She, like the rest of her generation, would settle for nothing less than perfection in their household chores. She had tried, bless her heart, to pass this determination onto me. That may have been her only failure. To Nana, cleaning was a mission. You did not clean by fits and starts. You cleaned thoroughly, obsessively. You systematically washed the tub, the sink, the toilet. You scrubbed the toilet bowl and made certain there was no lime-induced brown ring around the water line. You washed the mirror, the window and the floor with equal precision and only using the appropriate cleaning product. You left the room with it smelling disinfected and looking sparkling clean.

So, one day, as I was humming along downstairs with the vacuum, Nana was (unbeknownst to me) assembling her Comet, Tidy Bowl and Windex along with a platoon of buckets, rags, sponges and the toilet brush in preparation of her cleaning ritual. I'm not sure how she managed to gather all these things together without my knowing it. I do know that for the five months she lived here, she always managed to remember the crunched up cleaning rag that rested in the crook of water pipe under the sink. Right where she'd taught me to put it.

I was happily vacuuming away, lulled into a strange domestic calm induced by the thrum and vroom, while Nana and Rachel were enjoying their morning nap. Peace and cleanliness were just within my reach. I didn't hear any running water. I didn't hear bottles dropping. I didn't hear Rachel's squeals of delight which any real mother would have heard from two miles away.

After I finished, I felt I had earned a break. I wound the cord around and around with a little purr in my heart. I was about to have my ceremonial cup of coffee and maybe call a girlfriend when I first heard water running. I investigated the washing machine and the dishwasher. Nothing. Then I realized it was coming from upstairs. Did I leave the water running in my bathroom? Maybe Nana's forgetfulness was contagious.

I ran up the steps. I didn't even make it to the top before I saw a slow and steady trickle of water working its way down the stairs. The source of the trickle—quickly turning to steady stream—was a tipped over bucket on the top of the landing.

"What in heaven's name...?" Nana's words fell out of my mouth with such a natural ease that I knew I was slowly becoming her, and there was no escape. As the water streamed past my toes, I froze in a state of confusion.

Noise was emanating from the guest bathroom, so I walked there briskly tiptoeing in an effort to avoid the wet floor. There was Nana—or I should say—Nana's rump. She was on her hands and knees scrubbing the bathroom floor, as happy as I've ever seen her, at least from behind. Rachel in the tub with spigot running, held a rag and a sponge, tossed Comet into the air with abandon and sucked occasionally on the toilet brush. My toddler was fully clothed and covered with caustic substances from head to toe.

"Nana!"

She didn't respond, but Rachel giggled with delight.

"Nana, Nana, Naanaaa!" I totally lost my composure. I was supposed to be enjoying my ceremonial cup of coffee.

"What are you doing?" I asked, though upon reflection, it was a ridiculous question.

"Why, honey girl, I'm cleaning the bathroom," she said with a smile. Now my initial internal response was, "Awww, she's calling me 'honey girl.' She used to call me that all the time when I was growing up. Isn't that adorable?" But my sentimental brain was overruled by the disastrous vision in front of me. Nana, on the other hand, was as calm and settled as a priest performing a familiar Mass for the thousandth time.

"But what about the baby?" I cried.

"What about her?" she said gently.

"She's a mess, and...and...this is Comet, for God's sake!" I yelled.

"Stop swearing, honey girl."

My mind reeled. I wanted to scream, "You think this is swearing? I'll show you swearing. I'm a professional woman; I've worked in the corporate world; I can swear like a truck driver on a Friday night at a strip club."

"I put her in the bathtub, so she wouldn't go anywhere. We were just fine until you showed up," Nana said absently, while continuing to scrub away.

I removed Rachel from the tub and took off her toxic-covered clothing. I turned on the shower and began to rinse her off with the showerhead. She giggled and cooed and reveled in her bonding moment with Nana.

"See," Nana claimed as she sat up on her haunches, "now the shower's clean and so is the baby. A double duty."

I thought I should be angry. I felt angry, but I didn't really know why. Maybe it's because I didn't have complete control of the situation? Maybe it was because I'm sixty years younger and couldn't sit on my haunches that easily. When it came down to it, I knew why I was angry. I was angry because I thought *I* should decide when the bathroom got cleaned or if the baby got up from her nap. And I was certain that I was the one who should decide which toxic chemicals my daughter was allowed to play with. It was my call whether caustic fumes and abrasive materials should cover my daughter from head to toe, and I knew it was my right to choose her brand of pacifier and to decide whether or not that pacifier would be a toilet brush.

After a few moments of panic, I realized this was not the end of the world. I should be grateful that a 92-year-old woman wants to clean my bathroom (better than I ever would) and watch my child at the same time. No real harm was done, right?

I sighed and convinced myself that the bathroom fiasco was the worst that would probably happen. We finished the "cleaning" and moved on to lunch. Nana and Rachel were becoming fast friends. Or so I thought. Rachel had definite ideas about her life, and those ideas did not always mesh with Nana's ideas.

"No Nana," she would tell her, when Nana tried to feed her.

"She likes to do it herself," I said to my grandmother.

"No, Rachel," Nana stated when Rachel insisted on a bottle. "You're too old for that."

"We're not quite there yet, Nana," I said gently. "I'm trying."

"Well you're not trying hard enough, now are you?"

I let it go. I had to choose my battles.

If I had only known at the time that I was in a full scale war, I would have amassed more artillery, more ordnance, better planning. I would have spent more time with Sun Tzu's *The Art of War* as my bedside companion. As it was, my snoring husband did little to shore up my defenses.

So I let it go, and we moved on. As we entered the third week, I thought a trip to the enclosed warm and tiny local mall would be a nice winter outing. It seemed like such a good idea. A perfectly safe and fun activity. I mean, you can't leave the water running at the mall, right?

DAY 28

Dear Journal,

Did you notice that I didn't write anything last week? I am recovering. From the mall. Yes, it's taken me a week to recover.

The trip started out as a reprieve for us all. Freezing rain and harsh winds reduced us to staying inside. We all suffered from the "Febs." That's what my college friends used to call it. February cabin fever kills the spirit. There's no Christmas to look forward to and the blight of winter hovers ahead. That no-account spring hides far around the corner.

We are surrounded by bitter, cold, broken-down trees, brown lawns and dirty snow. The driveways are frozen over and too treacherous for the old and infirm. And it's dark for so many hours of the day. Dark when you wake up; dark until the sun comes up over the trees; and dark when the sun doesn't come out at all. Dark when you're just beginning to prepare dinner and dark long before you're ready for sleep. Maybe the Febs is really just another name for Seasonal Affective Disorder. The Febs is SAD.

So, of course, the mall called to us like the perfect diversion. A chance to turn the Febs upside down. A chance to be cheered by the bright artificial lights in hope that they might brighten our spirits as well. And that's how we all seemed to feel once we got inside.

Rachel was content to sit in her stroller, drink her bottle and take in the sights. Nana moved along slowly, totally aware that she was making a statement in her colorful clothes.

Ever since I can remember, Nana favored bright colors. I think that's why I ran right to her when we came home from the airport. I hadn't seen her since I was two-and-a-half, as Dad had been stationed in Germany. When he was killed in the crash, Mom just couldn't go to her own home. She couldn't be widowed, alone and pregnant and entertain five children all under the age of ten. I still have a hard time believing she survived to raise six happy kids.

I'm amazed that I would have remembered Nana at age four. But my mother tells me, and I do seem to have independent recollection of this, that as soon as we opened the door to Nana's house I ran to her, wrapped my chubby little arms around her, and said, "Hi'ya Nana!" And what I recall most vividly was her bright blue dress.

Bright colors infused Nana with happiness. I inherited this trait. Most of my closet is filled with reds and blues, pinks and neons. I love bright bold clothing, jewelry, and hats. And Nana and I, we adored our bling…the blingier the better.

As a child, I always knew Nana was synonymous with happiness, and her clothing, which included a dress, stockings and jewelry, reflected her jovial outlook as well as her penchant for order. I couldn't remember a time when I didn't see her waist-length hair swooped up into a neat bun accessorized with a matching ribbon and perky bow.

So there we were strolling through the mall on this dismal day, all feeling happy—me in my red coat and Nana in her hat du jour, a nude-colored braided affair. She looked vaguely like a bald person with a skin braid surrounding the crown of her head. Her coat was extraordinary—a full-length tapestry design in the brightest orange and gold brocade with a hint of burnt umber to complete the ensemble.

We shopped a little, taking our time. I wasn't really looking for anything in particular. This was meant to be an outing to make my babies tired. We wandered wherever our interest led us. Nana eyed some denture cream and lavishly spent on herself. Rachel became the proud owner of a new baby toothbrush which was thankfully a bit smaller than the toilet brush.

We dined for lunch at the food court. Rachel had chicken fingers and *fench fies.* I questioned my parenting at this juncture. I knew on every single level this was a mistake. I was certain that I was encouraging a life choice that would ruin her. But I just didn't care at that moment. I was reveling in the joy of making everyone happy and the absence of hissy fits. Nana had a fish sandwich and *fench fies*, too. When you're a Nana, you can eat whatever you damn well please. I had a piece of pizza. We were all deliriously happy with our food choices.

It was quite a nice outing for a dreary winter's day. Nana and I were talking about the times when my brothers and sisters and I were all little. It was a sort of a "do you remember?" duel. Her memory was amazing. I mean her long-term memory. I was about to find out her short-term memory was a different animal all together.

"Nana," I said, pushing the stroller past a cookie store, "do you remember how you used to keep all those silver dimes in that big apple cookie jar in your closet?"

"Of course, honey girl. Do you remember how you used to steal pennies out of the yellow milk money jar in the dining room?" she asked me with a raised eyebrow.

"Did you know that?"

She just laughed at me.

"I hated your slimy pot pie," I said to her, and stuck out my tongue in her direction.

She laughed again. "I know that, but your brothers loved it."

This was the essence of Nana. As long as the boys liked it, that was acceptable and in fact, always preferable. Men were to be catered to, coddled and preferred under all circumstances. Her sons and my brothers were extremely spoiled and often selfish. This made me crazy for many years. And certainly contributed to my arch-feminism.

My baby brother Bill *loved* Mrs. Schloerer's mayonnaise *so much more* than Hellmann's (the cheaper brand) that Nana would buy Hellmann's and put it in the Mrs. Scholerer's jar. Okay maybe that's not quite spoiling him, but she was still catering to his wishes. The rest of us would have gotten the Hellmann's and liked it. And she always qualified my legal career by saying I *worked* for a lawyer because she just couldn't wrap her mind around my *being* a lawyer and not a man at the same time. Ah yes, sexism at its finest.

But we were at the mall, so I put aside her tongue wagging and continued to enjoy the lazy winter outing. The afternoon was waning, and we were nearing that glorious time--their nap time. Right about then, I remembered that I needed a sympathy card. So on the way out, we stopped at the card store. Nana seemed a bit tired, so I sat her on the bench outside the Hallmark store with strict instructions.

"I am going to take Rachel and go in this store right here, Nana. Do not leave this bench until I come out. I'll be right back. This won't take five minutes."

She nodded her head. I was starting to feel a little guilty for staying so long at the mall. But to pack them up on another day just to get a card would have been ludicrous.

I entered the store with Rachel. Of course, the sympathy cards were way in the back of the store, so I couldn't keep my eye on Nana. I grabbed the first one I saw and pushed the stroller to the cashier. I paid for the card and triumphantly entered the mall.

Nana was gone.

I couldn't believe it. I looked at every bench as far left and as far right as I could see. No brocade anywhere. The educated professional that I am, I mentally examined the situation and formulated a plan. Then I completely ignored that plan and panicked. I ran with the stroller to one end of the mall. I didn't see Nana anywhere. I started down one of the offshoots of the mall and ran into a security guard.

"Excuse me," I said. I was breathless.

"Yes Ma'am!" barked the security guard. This is obviously the break she'd been waiting for. She was at attention and ready to secure. I hadn't even told her my problem yet.

"I seem to have lost my grandmother, and I was wondering…"

She released her walkie-talkie from the clasp on her belt. "We have a 16-22 here, all personnel, 16-22 alert!"

She looked at me carefully. I guess to make sure I'm wasn't the real perp returning to the scene of the crime. Rachel began to cry.

"Could you give us a description, ma'am?"

"She's 92 years old and she's wearing a gold and orange brocade coat."

"Her name, ma'am?"

"Margaret, her name is Margaret."

"Any other distinguishing marks?"

She is 92 and wearing a gold and orange brocade coat. Isn't this distinguishing enough? Through gritted teeth I said, "No, no other distinguishing marks. Please just get some help so we can look for her."

Rachel was really crying now. "Honey, what's the matter?"

"Poo, Poo, Mommy."

"Oh, please honey, not now."

Rachel continued to cry harder.

"I have to go change her diaper," I said to the security guard. "I'll be in the ladies room, and then I'll be looking for my grandmother. If you find her, I'll check at the mall office."

"10-4, Ma'am."

"Yeah, 10-4, whatever. Let's go Rachel."

The diaper changing went without a hitch. I gave Rachel the spare bottle of juice and she was happy once again. I was only buying a small window of happiness. She desperately needed her nap.

How could I lose my Nana? How far could she go? The mall was not that big. My mother will kill me. I resumed running through the mall. I covered every hallway. I looked in stores. I started crying. Rachel started crying. I was reasonably certain no one would kidnap her. And almost as certain that she wouldn't go off like an old dog to find a place to die. My heart was pounding. I was devastated. I checked with security. They hadn't found her. They suggested calling the police and told me to go home and wait. I wanted to leave this mall an hour ago. But I was determined to stay until hell froze over if that's how long it took to find my grandmother.

Then it hit me. Could it be possible? She knew we were about to leave. I ran to the end of the mall. Rachel was thrilled at the ride and began laughing hysterically. I, on the other hand, was sobbing hysterically. I ran through the glass doors and out into the parking lot. Halfway across the lot, I saw the gold and orange glint in the fading February light.

"What the hell are you doing?" I yelled across the parking lot. Everyone within five miles could hear me. I ran to the car. "I cannot believe you! What in God's name were you thinking? I have been looking everywhere for you."

"You said to go to the car, that we were leaving," Nana said. "What took you so long?"

That was last week, I don't expect to fully recover until next February.

DAY 30

We were moving along a little more smoothly. The routine of breakfast, short walks with Troon, and naptime resumed. Our days were full. At least my days were full. Rachel and Nana were becoming great friends. Nana would read to her, or they would watch television while I was making lunch.

Often, during this routine I was reminded of my childhood. Nana spent a lot of time talking to us while she cooked and cleaned and made the beds. We didn't talk about worldly topics or deep, dark secrets. We were just little. But she would tell us how to clean and make beds and get everything done in time to watch the TV game show "Concentration" over lunch. This was an important part of our childhood routine. When we solved the puzzle, host Art Linkletter would be so proud of us. "Concentration" made us feel competent and capable, and Art was a comforting daily companion. Cleaning, cooking and conversation really made the mundane miraculous. Often as I made their lunch, I would remember how Nana let me 'help' with chores. My favorite was cooking. Nana allowed us to get right in there and work alongside her. I didn't realize what a treat this had been for me as a child. I thought it was work. But as Nana began to engage Rachel in the kitchen, I realized that working side by side with an expert is a treat at any age.

Nana's cooking is legendary especially her pot pie. Lest you think you know what pot pie is and were wondering how it could be slimy, I assure you, you have no idea what real Pennsylvania Dutch pot pie is. It is not the Swanson's pie you buy in the frozen food department with rubber chicken, over-cooked peas and carrots soaking in gravy and settled in a flaky crust made with good lard so that you forget what you're really eating. No, this is the recipe for Nana's pot pie:

Pennsylvania Dutch Pot Pie

Stew a chicken. (Now this must be a "stewing chicken" and not a roasting chicken. A stewing chicken is old, sinewy and not good for much of anything but pot pie, but when done properly, men will kill for a night with a stewing chicken.)

After stewing a whole chicken, take it out of the pot. Remove the skin. Take the meat off the chicken. (And I think eating this is the disgusting part). Scoop the excess fat off the broth. But not too much because that's from whence the flavor emanates (and the fat continues to soften the chewy chicken while you cook the crap out of it).

Throw the chicken back in the pot of broth. Cook the crap out of it. While you let the chicken boil in the broth, cut up some celery, onions and a few carrots. Throw it in the pot and hope it helps.

Finally, you hand-make egg noodles from scratch. You place an egg in a well of flour and work the dough until it's just so. You shape and cut the dough into two inch squares. You give the raw dough to any child that happens to be "helping" to keep them entertained. Then you take this precious, delicious, home-made noodle that any expensive restaurant would kill for, and you throw it into the pot of slimy, rubbery chicken. Cook till the noodles are sufficiently smeared with grease and the broth has become opaque. Serve in a bowl like soup. My brothers loved it. And truth be told, it was delicious and healthy and made from scratch. I just didn't like it. So sue me. I ate it, like every other hungry kid in my house and was always wishing it was a Swanson's.

I refused to make anything like this for Rachel, but now that Nana was in my house, sometimes she insisted on cooking. I would plan meals which she could cook and Rachel would eat. Cheerios fit the bill. But Nana was adamant about being a bit more creative than that.

I would pull out my recipe cards and try to find something we could create as a team without wreaking too much havoc. I settled on Shoo-fly pie. You are beginning to wonder what planet I live on, aren't you?

Shoo-fly pie, another Pennsylvania Dutch favorite, was apparently born out of the need to get rid of flies. We could have made apie cakes (pronounced APE-ee), but they taste like molasses-flavored hockey pucks. I could just envision slap-shots around my kitchen floor.

So, I got out Nana's special pie plates, which she brought with her for just such an occasion. These pie plates were ceramic, dark brown with a lightly colored border. I am certain they were antique and most probably magic. Or maybe it was Nana who was magic. Whatever it was they made perfect pie. I wouldn't even suggest we use my pie plates, the P-word (Pyrex) which would be sacrilege. Yes, there were a whole host of words we couldn't use around Nana. These pie plates brought many a moan of joy to me and my brothers and sisters as we grew up. If you saw the pie plates on the counter before you went to school, or out to play on a Saturday after your chores, you knew that there was a delight to behold for dinner or breakfast the next day. Sure, you could have an apple pie for dinner, but you could have shoo-fly or apie cake for *breakfast* and how many times do you get pie for breakfast? Ah, those pie plates were always harbingers of happiness.

We assembled the flour, sugar, butter, eggs, brown sugar and molasses. We made the crust and gave gobs of dough to Rachel. She proceeded to eat it, wear it, and use it for spackle on the kitchen wall. Meanwhile, Nana instructed me on the fine art of rolling dough.

"Don't push too hard, honey girl, you'll make it tough," she told me. This was not new to me. She taught me how to make a pie when I was probably 12 or 13. The instructions were always the same.

"Okay," I said as I brushed flour from my hands to my face to get the hair out of my eyes. Hygiene was not a part of early twentieth century cooking.

"Here, let me do it," she said. She pushed me aside and grabbed the rolling pin. She had a pretty good push for an old broad.

"Fine!" I told her. This was probably the *exact* conversation from 20 years ago.

But boy could she roll with the best of them. The crust was just thin enough to work with, and it was also flaky to the core.

We blended the flour, sugar, brown sugar, and molasses by hand. We poured the ingredients into the pie crusts, which had been carefully placed in the plates. We fluted each crust border between fingers and thumb. Nana's flute was much more even and professional looking than mine. We sprinkled the sugary, cinnamon crumbs on top and placed our confections in the oven. Lord, the house smelled incredible. I forgot how much I missed the smell of sweet pies baking in my home.

My girls were pooped. I put them to bed and cleaned up the kitchen. I took the pies out of the oven just as my husband came in the front door.

"Wow, what smells so good?"

"Shoo-fly."

"Hey, maybe we'll keep Nana here forever."

If it only were as easy as pie.

DAY 35

Rachel had diarrhea. Nana was incontinent. I was spending every minute of my day cleaning up after these two girls. After just one month, I needed a vacation. The phone rang. I answered it, "Shit Palace." Thank God, it was my sister, although, at that moment I really didn't care. I wanted the whole world to know what I was dealing with. This was harder than I thought it would be. I still had four months to go before Nana would go home. I felt like a shitheel. That was one of my grandmother's favorite terms, when she thought we weren't listening.

My grandmother gave up her entire retirement to care for my siblings and me, and I was whining about a few months. I needed a grateful check but it was hard to find one between the dirty diapers, the shitty bathroom floor, and the seven loads of sheets in the laundry. Mentally, I tried some creative 'grateful' mantras:

"I love the color brown."

"I, myself, am healthy and in control of my bladder."

"I don't have to record billable hours for cleaning."

"I hate this shit." Oh wait, that's not the right mantra. I realized I was saying this out loud...and saying "shit" a bit too much when I heard Rachel pipe up, "Mommy, I full of shit."

Was I now a bad parent?

Shit.

DAY 42

I found them both eating the dog's food.

Every time I gave them a little rope, they would hang me. Yes, it had become "me" and "them."

I was upstairs for a second—for a millisecond. I came back downstairs with a load of laundry. The never-ending load of laundry. And there they were. Nana was sitting on the couch. Rachel was standing in front of her—the two of them unreservedly smiling at one another with great joy. Nana was shaking her fist, like you would if you were about to throw the dice in craps. This was how she ate peanuts and M&M's. You shake a little. You throw a few in your mouth. You shake a little and do it all over again. Rachel was imitating her. I knew I didn't have any peanuts in my house. Peanuts were chokers of small children. Peanut allergies were like Sarin gas to toddlers. I kept that out of my house until I was sure I wouldn't inadvertently kill anyone. I couldn't think of one edible commodity in my kitchen that would qualify for this game. And I realized, they were chewing.

So I said, "Nana, what are you eating?"

She held out her hand and opened it.

"Nana, that's DOG FOOD!"

She turned to me as calmly as can be, pointed to Rachel and said with all justification:

"She's eating it."

I looked at the two of them in wonder. Troon looked at them in puzzlement. The dog hovered around them, hoping that they would drop one of these treats so he could gobble it right up. I didn't have the heart to tell Troonie there was a full dish of that stuff in the next room just waiting for him.

I closed my jaw and thought for a moment. "Is dog food nutritional? Is this better than candy or peanuts? Will I be arrested?"

"Knock yourself out," I said and left the room.

DAY 45

It seemed as if I was alone in this caregiving of two people almost a century apart, and I was. I didn't have any other mom in my playgroup caring for her grandmother although there were one or two "sandwiches" whose mothers or fathers aged rapidly with one disease or another and were fighting similar battles.

I was a child of the original "sandwich generation." When we moved in with Nana, we squeezed five children, my grandparents, my great-grandmother and my mom into a row home or half-a-double with three bedrooms and one bath. Imagine a family doing that now. Yet, my childhood best friend four doors down, Beth Ann, was also living with her mother and grandmother. The neighbors with the big, sprawling farmhouse and backyard where we played ball also lived with their grandmother. This was not a new phenomenon; we were just better at whining about it.

My great-grandmother died just a few days after we moved in with Nana. She was always clever like that. My grandfather, Pop-Pop, who I adored, was a boisterous, song-singing alcoholic. He died three years later in 1964, in a car accident. He was our male role model. I loved that white-haired, Mummer-singing, manly-man. My little sister was petrified of him. In this time before car seats and even seat belts, my Pop-Pop would take my baby brother riding in the car. This petrified my mother, but only joy came of it. He fed us hot dogs for Sunday breakfast. He bought us boxes of York Peppermint Patties—boxes—not just one for each. I was never so sad as when York Peppermint Patties changed their wrappers. It stole a memory from me. But the smell still suggests Pop-Pop is just around the corner singing "Oh dem golden slippers."

Pop-Pop died two days before Thanksgiving, and being compassionate, understanding children, we were stunned when my mother and Nana said they didn't want to cook a Thanksgiving feast. Luckily for us, those were the days when the corner grocery knew all of its customers and provided that feast for us free of charge.

Those of us in the sandwich phase were noosed with guilt when we even thought of complaining about the challenges we faced. I might argue that the pace and speed of our lives gave us the benefit of more whining. But how absurd was that? The chores were the same. We had more conveniences and allegedly more free time. But the downside hadn't changed. It was drudgery, time-consuming and boring. Being a homemaker challenged the mind, body and spirit every single day to stick with it, find the rewards, and reap them.

Today I received one little reward. I was tired. I was always tired. Once in a great while instead of trying to beat the system, I would join it. I took a nap when they did. Usually, I would try to complete between one and fifty tasks, playing "Beat the Clock" until they woke up. Because, as every other mother knew, I never knew when they would wake up.

But this day, I just had to take a nap. I could not look at one more dirty sheet, towel, shirt or pair of pants. I did not want to put dishes away, shovel ice off the driveway, pay bills or even watch TV. I wanted to rest, really rest. So when I heard both of their rhythmic breaths coming through the monitor, I tiptoed to my room, closed the door and put myself to bed.

Sometime during this process, it started to snow. It stayed quiet for some time. I fell into a very deep sleep. The kind of sleep that when you're dreaming, you think you're awake, but on some level you know you are still sleeping. It felt good. It felt heavy like six or seven quilts cuddling my tired brain.

I was laughing in my dreams and so were Nana and Rachel. This woke me with a start. They really were laughing. I grabbed my glasses, threw off the covers and ran down the hall. I could see the snowflakes falling as I passed the windows. The driveway was just covered with the dust of a new snow. Neither of the girls were in their beds.

I heard laughter through the monitor, but coming from downstairs. I ran. I had committed the unpardonable sin of a caregiver; I fell asleep on my watch.

I reached the family room, and there they were watching a Barney tape together and drinking hot chocolate. I tried to appear calm.

"Uh, hi guys," I stammered, "watcha' doin'?"

"We watch Barney, Mommy!" yelled Rachel.

"Yeah! I see that. Why didn't you wake me up?"

"You were so tired, honey girl, and we were just fine. Rachel knew how to turn on the tape. So we made some cocoa and watched TV."

"Oh my God, Nana. Thank you so much. I really was tired."

"I know sweetie, don't you think I don't."

"Shhh," said Rachel, "Barney singin."

I love you. You love me. We're a happy family. And yes, we were. For that moment we were just perfect.

DAY 50

Today we took my sister for chemotherapy.

In my family this is how it goes. Cindy was the pretty one. Tina was the smart one, Caren was the cute one, Chip was the ladies' man, Bill was the baby, and I'm the one with the personality. I often thought that was because they ran out of things to say, but that's not logical since I'm a middle child. But truth be told, I'm sure it's because like the quintessential middle child, I never stopped talking or seeking attention. Nevertheless, Cindy really was beautiful. She had stunningly gorgeous long black hair that I used to iron for her when we were in high school. She had a pixie face, and a cute figure. She had a mean sense of humor and a mean streak to boot. She smoked, but it was not lung cancer that grabbed her; it was breast cancer.

By the time Rachel was born, Cindy had already had her first mastectomy. In order to be considered "cured" of breast cancer, you have to have a five-year cancer-free diagnosis. We were now in year one-and-a-half and that sucker would not go away. My mother was Cindy's primary driver for chemo, but my stepfather needed to go to their Florida home. "Needed" actually means "wanted," but since Mom was his wife, she had to go too. My mother was raised to do as her husband wished, so off they went. I readily volunteered to take Cindy to chemotherapy. This was not a duty. This, too, was a labor of love. I wanted to share this with her in every way I could. She needed me to watch and listen and learn. I needed her to get better. And I wanted to know everything I could about breast cancer, for her, for me, for my sisters, my daughter and my friends.

A little knowledge is a dangerous thing. It's horrible. And yes, I did bring the orange-brocaded Nana and the snow-suited toddler along. It actually helped. They were hysterical and ridiculous. All the patients cooed over Rachel. They didn't get too many toddlers down here in the cancer center, thank God. And Nana and Cindy always had a special relationship. They were both very funny people. We all were, with the exception of my mother. She seems to be missing her sense of humor. I mean, she knows what's funny—she knows when to laugh, but she isn't funny. And yet, at any family gathering, we kids were always laughing hysterically. We often had our mother peeing in her pants. Sometimes she was the brunt of our jokes. But we all were targets; no one was spared. We liked it that way.

The cancer center was in the basement of the local hospital. You walked down cold linoleum hallways. You wound past the cafeteria and the testing rooms and tucked back in the corner was the treatment area for the cancer patients. It felt like we were hiding something. Like in "Terms of Endearment" where everyone was whispering, "She's got cancer." It's bad enough that your head is bald, you are puking, and you want to pretend you are leading a normal life. But you are even a pariah in the hospital. They should change this. Put the cancer patients right up front. "See, we're treating for cancer. Are you brave enough to do this?"

We sat in the basement and made jokes with Cindy while she sat in the big pink chair having the chemo burn through her veins. She didn't have enough vein power anymore, so they had placed a "port" in her chest. This was lovely. They pulled tubing out of her bra and hooked her up to the bag of chemicals, and pulled the pretty pink curtains around her so she could fry in comfort.

I was happy to be here with her, but I wanted to puke. Rachel was a bit difficult to contain. They had toys and books for children, which was a kind of grace. But it was also the saddest thing you could imagine. Nana read to Rachel and played with the toys. Cindy and I talked about the bygone days of her luxurious hair and when it would return.

The nurses were amazing. I hated her doctor. He was old-fashioned. "Yeah, you have cancer, blah, blah, blah. This is what we'll do to fix it." His cancer patients didn't get "bedside manner."

But the nurses—oh, the nurses. They brought treats, they talked about their families and they remembered everything about these patients. They knew how patients would react to certain drugs, and they knew how strangers would react to their patients on the street staring at their scarf-enslaved heads. They had a sympathetic cluck for all of it. I loved them. They were sisters, mothers, friends, all in the battle, on the front line, all the time.

It was sweet syrup to her to hear Nurse Debbie tell Cindy that the adriomyacin (chemo) would not be every week anymore. It burns as it goes in your veins and it burns coming out as vomit.

Then there was Peggy. She was in charge of everyone and everything. Often, I wished she were the doctor. I swore she knew ten times more than any of these physicians. And she told you what she knew. She didn't candy coat it either. For us, this was critical. We wanted to know. We wanted to know everything. How long would Cindy be on chemo? How much would it hurt? How would it hurt? How would you know if it was working? These weren't questions; these were demands for information. Peggy told you everything she knew. She did it quietly, with authority and reason. She told you things you didn't think to ask like if you had to be admitted to the hospital, you should bring that pink plastic bucket and all the stuff in it back with you or they'll charge you for it again and again and it's not covered by insurance. You think a doctor would tell you that? You would think a doctor would know that? Maybe he had more important things to do, but it was indeed those little things that made Cindy feel like a person and not just a chemo patient.

Nana was affably quiet and quite the babysitter during this hour or so. She sort of became the "Nana-in-the-room." Not like the 500-lb. gorilla, but like the fairy godmother who suddenly appeared to let you know everything was going to be alright. People were surprised to see her in the waiting room, especially with a toddler. When they realized she was just a visitor and she engaged them in quiet, calm, grandmotherly conversation, she too was like the soothing nurses. Huh. Who would've guessed that?

After chemo, we went out for lunch. Cindy puked, Rachel threw her food and Nana drooled soup down her dress. A regular power lunch.

DAY 53

Yesterday was pretty harsh. We needed a "chill day." I decided to just stay home and do nothing, worry about nothing. I figured, I'd do a little laundry, maybe take the two of them for a quick walk up and down the driveway, and then it would be naptime.

Back upstairs I went. This pattern of leaving the two gremlins alone had not yet revealed to me that it was always a disaster waiting to happen. I was humming as I sorted the darks from the whites, the whites from the mediums. You know "mediums" doesn't really fit as a description. It's more a size.

Crash! Oh, holy shit! I ran down stairs. Nana was crying, Rachel was crying. I'm yelling. "What? What happened?"

"I'm sorry, honey girl, I didn't mean it."

"Mean what? What happened?"

I still couldn't find anything wrong. Clearly, there was no blood and no broken bones, so how bad could it be?

"I was just trying to help."

I picked up Rachel to calm her down.

"Shh, honey, it's okay, it's okay. Stop crying. Mommy's here."

I fought with every breath I had to keep calm and not scream, "What the fuck!?"

So much for chilling out.

I said, "Okay, Nana, tell me what happened."

"I dropped the laundry soap."

The laundry soap?

"That's not so bad."

"It knocked over the vacuum cleaner."

"Oh, that was the crash, okay?"

"And broke the hose on the washing machine."

"Whaaatttt?"

I ran to the laundry room and sure enough the water was rushing out like Niagara Goddamn Falls.

The gnashing of teeth and wailing resurged and the Superfund cleanup began. My husband came home to this amazingly pristine house and was agog at how clean and fresh smelling this house could be in just one afternoon.

A side note. In the twenty years or so my grandmother and mother spent raising six children, I never once heard a swear word come out of their beautiful mouths. The worst thing my alcoholic grandfather ever said was "goddamn" or "hell". Never once did any grownup resort to swearing in their frustration. Can you believe it? Six children, an alcoholic and two women living in a tiny house and not one swear word? I kept forgetting that these women were my real role models. Not the women with truck-driver mouths in law school who trained me for the corporate world. Almost every day I swore (how's that for irony?) that I was going to <u>stop</u> swearing, and I would lose the battle. Every day, I lost the battle. I needed to try harder. How did my mother and grandmother do that? Six kids, every day, tiny house and no swearing. A miracle, I thought.

DAY 54

Oh the days were just flying by.

DAY 56

Every month or so my girlfriends and I had a Sunday brunch. We used to do this at a restaurant, but we were so noisy and stayed so long that we were asked to leave one too many times. Consequently, we started having brunch at each other's houses, depending on whose husband was out of town, who could watch the kids, etc. These brunches were long, involved affairs. We had so much to talk about, so many world issues to solve, that we needed at least four or five hours around the council table. Our husbands were aghast that a "brunch" could take more than an hour or two. They couldn't imagine what we were doing. I thought that, at first, each husband thought his wife must be having an affair or becoming addicted to gambling. But when we brought the brunches into our respective homes, and we were just talking, talking, talking with no end in sight, most of their fears were allayed.

These were more than gab fests. We discussed politics, money, world affairs, child rearing, and spent an inordinate amount of time on the controversial subjects in the latest People Magazine issue. We were all annual subscribers to "the Bible." Of course, we would probably be able to go to Hollywood with the money we would make if we spent as much time discussing and making investments as we did on Julia Roberts, Tom Cruise and Nicole Kidman. Nonetheless, this brunch was a critical time for all of us, and it contributed greatly to the continuing sanity we were able to maintain in a world spiraling ever-downward.

It was my turn to host just such a brunch. We didn't stick to the "your turn, my turn" rule. Our home lives were all very different, and so whoever could make it go that month took a turn. With Nana here, I should have declined, but I wanted to take a turn. Or maybe I had some crazy death wish. Intellectually, I thought it made sense to have the brunch here because I could put Rachel down for her nap and maybe Nana too. But I think I was really playing emotional roulette. I wanted to see if I really could be Supermom, Supergranddaughter and Superfriend—all in the same day. What is this compelling notion of my generation to place obstacles in our way for certain failure? I think I was just competing with Paula Zahn who was in the latest issue of People who raised her kids, ran 30 miles a week and was an avid skier. Oh yeah, and a beautiful, intelligent woman as well. I'd show her. It never occurred to me that Paula Zahn might have had a bit of help on the home front—and I didn't mean her husband.

The brunch menu did not require extensive cooking preparation. The hostess could choose as simple a menu as bagels, lox and cream cheese with a bit of fruit, or as complex as a chocolate soufflé with crème fraiche and raspberry chutney. Guess what I chose? Wrong. What nut would make a soufflé with Nana and Rachel running around the house. I did, however, concede to make a quiche—another French word, so it sounded like an exotic work of art—which caused very little distress, since I sneaked a frozen pie crust into the house without my grandmother seeing it. Just this one time, I promised

In order to get the house ready before my friends came, I would either have had to get up in the dark to beat Nana out of bed or set the table at ten o'clock the night before and make the raw quiche, put it in the refrigerator and bake it in the morning. I chose the latter because I wasjust not a get-up-at-the-crack-of-o'dark kind of gal. This all went swimmingly well. By 7:30 A.M., I came downstairs, after a glorious night's sleep and turned on the oven for baking.

Nana was at the kitchen table with her usual suspects of toast and coffee. But her curiosity was piqued.

"Honey girl, what's going on?"

"Why whatever do you mean, Nana, darling?" I replied. Somehow I had morphed into a British Dame preparing for the arrival of her bridge club with the utmost cool and collected manner. This was short-lived.

"What are you cooking?" Nana asked.

"I am baking a quiche. I put it together last night while you were in bed, so I wouldn't bother anyone this morning."

"Oh honey girl, I could have helped you with that. At least I could have made a good crust for you."

Like I could have really kept that frozen crust a secret. She didn't miss a trick.

"Did you remember that my girlfriends are coming for breakfast this morning?" I asked her in hopes that this didn't start one of those "you never told me that" debates.

"You never told me that."

I remained calm. This was a proud moment for me. The calmness, I mean. All of the first-world nations and their second-world sisters would have been proud. I firmly believed that impatience with the elderly was and is a worldwide epidemic. And I, for one, was going to do my part to remain calm and refuse to contribute to the spread of disease.

"Okay, well I'm sorry about that. But I need you to go and get changed because they will be here around 9:30. And then we can all have a nice breakfast together."

"I already had my breakfast," she said.

"Well, yes, I know that but by the time my friends come and we chat and have coffee, it will almost be time for lunch, and so you can call it that, okay?"

With a smile plastered on my face, I quickly rushed to the coffee pot. The mention of the word coffee made me realize the stimulant was missing from my body and would now miraculously have the opposite effect. The coffee would calm me down in the face of the impending argument.

"But..." Nana tried to interrupt.

"Just go get dressed, Nana, please," I cut her off. "We'll discuss what we call your next meal later."

"You don't have to get testy, honey girl," she said in a snit.

"Testy? Testy?"

Oops. She was right. I didn't have to get testy, but it was now 8:54 A. M. and they would be here soon. And for some reason, Rachel was still sleeping.

"Look, I'm sorry, Nana, I'm just getting a little wound up because my friends will be here soon, and I'm not quite ready, and Rachel hasn't even gotten up yet."

"If you drink less coffee, maybe you wouldn't be so jittery," she said as she ascended the stairs.

Of course, at that very moment, Rachel awakened with her mantra: "Mommy, come get me." Rather than fight with her too, I went to her room and quickly got her face washed, teeth brushed, and changed her diaper. I picked out an outfit and put it on her bed as I went to get her undershirt, socks and shoes.

"I don' like that dress, Mommy," she said.

"Oh honey, not today. Please just wear it for Mommy because her friends are coming to see how pretty you are." This, of course, is against all the rule books about building self-esteem in your daughter and preventing a future of anorexia and bulimia.

"I wear this, Mommy," she said proudly.

Out of her closet she pulled the ugliest, rattiest, too-small, hand-me-down from her favorite cousin that I stuffed at the bottom of the closet among the old shoes, discarded stuffed animals and dust bunnies so she wouldn't find it. I couldn't give up the battle. I am Supermom. I would never allow my daughter to be presented at a social function looking like Madonna in the '80's.

"No, Rachey, not today, please," I begged her.

She started to cry and throw the mother of all hissy fits. Toddlers absolutely without a doubt *know* when you are stressed beyond the max. They are equipped with "surrender radar." All toddlers know where and when you will give in for the sake of moving on. They are better negotiators than the highest priced lawyer in the swankiest Manhattan law firm.

"Okay!" I shout, "just get dressed."

Nana appeared in her *other* house coat. Apparently, this was getting dressed for company as well.

"What are you wearing?" I asked her accusingly.

"What would you like me to wear, your highness?" she answered as she stuck out her tongue.

I looked at Rachel and she was imitating her mentor. I stuck my tongue out at them too. Now I had two choices here. First, I could run crying to my room and slam the door. Second, I could break up in hysterical laughter and defuse this situation and try and start over. The fact that I *realized* that I had two choices is in and of itself an amazing response. So, I chose to laugh. It worked for me. We were all laughing and I didn't care what they wore. A life lesson. The door bell chimed and the troops from Orphan Annie filed down the stairs to greet our guests.

These particular friends were from my community theater group that I joined at the urging of my husband. I was originally a theater major in college and when I realized I would probably have a life of abject starvation if I continued on that path, I switched my major and went to law school. My group of theater friends arrived to breakfast with appropriate drama. Three of us starred in the first production I was in after my husband encouraged me to stop doing theater drive-bys and actually go in and audition. Even though it was just a few years ago, it seemed like a lifetime. We had become extremely close and extremely dependent upon one another for truth, justice and good companionship.

Sally was the special-ed school teacher. She was in her late 30's and single. She led a charmed life. At least that's what I chose to believe. Someone had to live it, so I had something to sigh about. She had somehow managed to rent a quaint old farmhouse and turned it into a place of warmth and welcome. She was the queen of party-givers. Terri was the shy one. She worked behind the scenes at the theatre—a thankless job. Yet she did thankless jobs as a master of organization, a kind-hearted soul and more generous with her time than anyone I knew. Because she was statuesque, organized, and bright, people often mistook her shyness for snobbery. We were ever grateful that somehow we learned to break through that exterior for the gift of her friendship behind it.

Lisa is....well, Lisa. She was the consummate actress. She had worked professionally, and the entire world was missing out on a bequest by not enjoying her talent. She was funny, wacky, crazy, and had amazing insight into people and their character. She entertained us endlessly and without her we would have lost the sparkle of this group.

These get-togethers were loud, obnoxious, full of laughter and cathartic, the great joy of friendship that allows you to rip the world wide open with sarcasm, political incorrectness and fun.

Now add Nana to this mix.

Sally and Terri were so sweet with Nana. Their mothers were in their seventies so they were not too far removed from what was happening with the elderly population. Lisa, on the other hand, had no grandmothers in her life and saw her parents on a limited basis. Lisa feared that Nana was some spectral being placed on this earth to haunt her. Nana's puttering, shuffling, teeth-dropping, and non sequiturs unnerved her. The rest of us found this amusing and were wont to misbehave with the cards that have been dealt here.

I managed to get Nana and Rachel settled in front of the television with some snacks and Nana's ever beloved crossword puzzle. This should have kept them at bay for at least an hour. In the dining room, Sally, Terri, Lisa and I were boisterous and jangled on free-flowing coffee.

The fun took an interesting turn as Nana entered the dining room.

"You girls are noisy," she said.

"We're sorry, Nana," said Terri, "why don't you join us?"

"C'mon," Sally joined in, "let's hear what you've got to say on the topic of men."

"Oh honey girl, I don't have much to say about that. I haven't used one of those for a very long time."

Howls of laughter ensued. I heard Rachel whining in the next room.

"What's the matter, honey?" I asked her.

"You friends too loud, Mommy. I can't hear Barney. Don't like bunch, Mommy."

"Okay, okay, Mommy's sorry. We'll try to behave ourselves. Do you want to stay here and watch Barney or do you want to come in the dining room with Mommy and her friends?"

"I watch Barney; just kreep kriet."

I snuggled her up with lots of blankets and a pillow on the couch. She hugged her stuffed animals and went back to TV mode. I thought she might be working on a little snooze if we could just be quiet in the other room. Fat chance.

I returned to the dining room where Nana has placed herself right next to Lisa. Lisa looked like a deer in the headlights. Terri and Sally were enjoying Nana's company as well as Lisa's discomfort. This is what true friendship is about—torturing each other.

"Nana, what are you talking about?" I asked her.

"I don't know."

Everyone chuckled.

"No, I mean what are you telling the girls?"

"Oh, I was telling them about the theater I worked in. They told me they were your theater girlfriends."

"That's right, Nana," said Terri, "now tell us about the purple velvet curtain."

"Oh honey girl, when I worked in that movie theater, the Hippodrome, they had the most beautiful lavender velvet curtain you would ever want to see. It was just tremendous. It covered the entire stage from end to end. I worked in that theatre for fifteen years as the cleaning lady. People treated that theatre like a pig sty. You wouldn't believe the things I found up in the balcony when I was washing the floors."

"What kind of things?" Sally asked.

"Oh you know, cigarette butts, candy wrappers, used tissues and those man things."

"'Man things'?" Lisa ventured.

Nana turned directly to Lisa and said:

"Sure, you know, the rubber things he uses to keep a girl from getting pregnant?"

"Oh God, you mean…?" Lisa sputtered.

"Yep, used ones too," Nana said matter-of-factly.

The rest of us burst into laughter, and Nana sat there with a smirk on her face. I couldn't have made a better set-up if I had practiced with Nana all day long for a week.

"Well, girls, I should look in on the baby. You have a good time. And try to keep it down, I think Rachel was trying to take a little nap."

She waggled her fingers as she left the dining room.

"Toodle-oo!"

Lisa gulped her coffee.

"I don't think I could do what you're doing. How do you keep her entertained? How do you keep from going crazy?" Lisa asked.

"It's not so bad," I lied.

"While you were out, she took out her teeth to show us how to whistle."

I spit my coffee out of my mouth. Terri and Sally nodded with laughter.

"That's just how it is, Lisa. If Rachel or Nana feel the need to engage in some kind of inappropriate bodily function in public—or private for that matter—I just deal with it and go on."

"Yeah, well, I'm never getting old." said Lisa. "It's too creepy and scary."

"Good luck with that," we all chimed in.

DAY 57

When I became a stay-at-home mom, I thought the time would fly by. Trying to balance work and a baby was overwhelming to me and there weren't enough hours in the day. I went back to my small town law firm six weeks after Rachel was born, and just couldn't bear to be away from her. I feel no differently now. I have the ultimate respect for those women who must work and raise their children, especially if they are single moms. I truly have the same respect for those moms who are better moms because they work outside the home. I didn't have any desire to return to the firm. But I sure as heck (no swearing today) missed adult conversation and confirmation.

Most of my clients were very kind to me. I was the Sally Field of lawyers. I was astounded and so were they, that we really did like each other. I had a real affinity for the elderly. I loved them. I loved their stories. I really loved their history; they have all lived in extremely interesting times. I even loved their plodding and prodding. My meetings with elderly clients were slow and easy. No rushing in or out the door. They weren't in a hurry to get to anything else, and I respected that neither should I. Sometimes it would try my patience. But not often. We would talk—really talk—about their legal issues. Should they disinherit certain children, should they put their children's names on their houses, their bank accounts, their CD's (money, not music) and I would give them honest answers.

I made a concerted effort never to condescend to these clients. They were smart, but frightened of a system they didn't understand, and up until this point, had no use for. They just wanted to be heard. I missed that. I was respected and privy to important information. One client told me this amazing story about how her husband of fifty years proposed to her through her father-in-law, while his son was stationed in Europe during World War II. I loved that stuff.

But the truth of the matter was, I really didn't miss the work. I <u>was</u> working all day every day. And I didn't really want to return to that work plus this work. I just wanted and craved a different viewpoint on a daily basis. I wanted some grown-ups around me. I wanted some fresh and lively conversation other than "what do you want for lunch?"

So we joined a playgroup. Nana couldn't sit on the floor or play in the McDonald's play land, but I took her anyway. I thought she would like a play group. But these were not her friends. She adored the little ones, but they overwhelmed her with their screaming and running and falling. She didn't care about the mental stimulation; I did. Nana was mostly content to drink her coffee and watch, but she would quickly burn out on the noise and flying French fries. I, on the other hand, needed these Moms to help assuage the fear of losing all forms of intelligence gained through expensive education. It became a Mexican standoff.

"Honey girl, I want to go home," she would say ever so politely.

"Okay, Nana, in just a minute," I would respond with equal equanimity.

Five minutes later. "Honey girl, I'm tired," she would say so that the other mothers could hear her.

"Oh, no you're not, you just got up from a morning nap," I would comment a bit too loudly.

Two minutes later. "Honey girl?" she would do in a stage whisper.

"Yes?" I would stage whisper in return.

"I beshit myself."

X gets the square.

DAY 60

It was getting very cold. We were expecting to have a doozy of a blizzard in the next day or so. My husband was out of town. My driveway was 787-feet long. We would be trapped or in the alternative, I would be required to figure out how to use the snow blower and remove 787 feet of blizzard while they napped. Have you ever heard a snow blower? Do you know how long it takes to snowblow 787 feet? It takes about two or three hours depending upon wind velocity, ice formation, wetness of snow and your own personal stamina.

Surely, we would be trapped. Like all other panicking young mothers and the elderly, we made the requisite emergency trip to the grocery store. This is where you skillfully dodged all the bread, eggs, and milk flying off the shelves as you navigated the store. My sister, Maggie, insists that bread pudding must be the emergency casserole for all blizzards because every cart and handbasket always contains these major ingredients.

We wended our way through the aisles. I had the same conversation in aisles 4, 9, and 13:

"Mommy?"

"Yes, Rachel?"

"Can I have cookies?"

"Okay, what kind?" "This kind."

She picked up those pink wafery things that look and taste like strawberry cardboard.

"No, not those," I said.

But one look at her crestfallen face told me to choose a different battle.

"Okay," I said.

Less than five minutes later.

"Mommy, can I have those?"

She pointed to the Fruit Roll Ups.

"No, honey they're too yucky," I told her.

"Not yucky, Mommy, YUM-MY," she says gumming her "M's" very emphatically so that I could perceive the distinction.

"No sweetie, you already have cookies, remember?"

"Don't want cookies, Mommy, want YUM-MY."

"No, Rach."

I pushed the cart as fast as I could to get to the next aisle. As I rounded the corner to the Mexican food—a safe bet—I saw Nana ambling as quickly as she could after me.

"Sorry, Nana."

"Honey girl?"

"Yes, Nana?"

"I need denture cream."

"Okay, it's a few aisles over."

I realized that I couldn't be here forever. I made it quickly through the canned goods, dog food and meat. But I had to have toilet paper. There was no way around it. I could not be snowed in for two days without enough toilet paper. It was a crucial purchase, yet a dangerous one, because it was near frozen foods: ice cream, pizza, and tater tots. I could sit Nana down at the pharmacy and rush through the last few things, but we all know that that was not a risk worth taking. Nana was moving slower. Damn, I should have done breads, baked goods, dairy, and frozen foods first. Now I am doomed. It was getting close to naptime.

I got lucky. There was a sale on Charmin, and it was on the end of the aisle. I grabbed a big package of twelve soft, cuddly rolls of toilet paper.

"Here, Rachel; hold this," I put her little arms around the edges and hid her face from the frozen foods.

Rachel started to giggle.

"No, Mommy, too big."

"Sure, you can hold it. You're a big girl now."

I crouched down and began to push the cart, effectively hiding little eyes from the bagel bites, pizzas, and ice cream.

"You funny, Mommy."

Then Nana piped up.

"Oh look, Rachel, it's those pizzas you like!"

"Pizza, Mommy, pizza, Mommy!"

I am absolutely convinced that Nana was jealous that I was paying attention to Rachel and not to her, so she jinxed me.

"Grrrr," I said to Nana.

"Okay," I said to them, "one more thing and one more thing *only*. Pizza or ice cream?"

"Honey girl, I want ice cream," Nana said matter-of-factly. "I like butter pecan."

"Eeeewww, no putter becan. Pizza, pizza, pizza," says Rachel.

"Okay," I said quite a bit too loudly," ice cream for you and pizza for you. That's it."

We made it around the rest of the aisles without much fanfare. We got out to the car. I buckled them in to their seats. I put all the bags in the trunk and returned the cart to the holding tank. I got in the car, took a deep breath, pulled out of the parking lot, and when we were halfway home, with Rachel sound asleep in her car seat, Nana turned to me and said,

"Honey girl?"

"Yes, Nana?"

"I think you forgot my denture cream."

"Oh hell, Nana, why didn't you say anything?" I said with exasperation.

"Because you said one more thing only," she said innocently.

"Oh hell," Rachel said in her sleep.

DAY 61

We had to go to the hospital to ensure that Nana would get a blood transfusion because her circulation was so poor. She was cold all the time. Apparently, this had something to do with her lack of Vitamin B and her diverticulitis and who the hell knows what else. I don't know why this is what we did when she was cold. But the doctor and my Mom, who is a nurse, told me that's what was to be done, so I took her. The whole process would only take a few hours. With the storm coming, I wanted to get this over with, so that Nana would be feeling well, especially if we were going to be housebound for a few days. On the other hand, did I really want her perky with cabin fever? I mulled this over for a while. It would have been completely selfish of me to delay her treatment just so she would be lethargic and compliant. Or would it? Guilt got the best of me, and I did the right thing; we trekked to the hospital.

Blood transfusions turned out to be a respite for us all. Nana got undivided attention, and I got to go home, put Rachel down for a nap and take one myself. Who cares about the goddamn laundry? I'm going to be snowbound for days; I could wash until my hands fell off, but the nap was great for everyone. You really don't appreciate the restorative powers of sleep until you are so deprived that you actually notice what a great invention sleep is.

We picked up Nana at the hospital. Wow! Everyone should get a blood transfusion once in a while. She was practically dancing down the aisles. So home we went and put on the stereo. If you knew Nana over the years, you would know that dancing was crucial to her well being. She would dance all the time. She was always the life of the party. As children, our house had plenty of music on the stereo and dancing was like watching TV. You just did it. And Nana was no slouch. She would join in, no matter the music or the time of day. In those days, if you put music on everyone had to listen. There were no iPods or even Walkmans. Music was a shared experience, whether you liked it or not. So we shared Mitch Miller sing alongs, Quiet Village instrumentals, Ray Coniff, Herb Alpert and the Tijuana Brass—and as my Mom got more modern—Peter, Paul and Mary. So there was a healthy dose of music and dancing going on in our little half-a-double, and Nana was right in there. Nana was not a particularly good dancer; she was a particularly happy dancer. And, like her grandchildren, her sense of humor was unparalleled. We were laughing and having a good time. As Rachel began to imitate Nana's dance moves, I started to wonder if she would grow up to dance like Elaine in *Seinfeld*.

DAY 62

The blizzard arrived. It was so beautiful. We were stranded in the woods surrounded by vanilla-covered trees. It was astounding. We barely had to turn on lights because the snow was so blinding in its whiteness. We were silent and reverential. We were quiet. We didn't turn on the television for hours. We just watched and listened to the falling snow. The crimson cardinals shocked us with their color in the bird feeder. Rachel squealed with delight to see the gash of red against the white, white, white. Nana and I smiled at one another. We have watched birds together many times.

Nana was a bird watcher from way back. The window in our tiny kitchen in our tiny house, in our tiny town, was minute. We would look out onto the postage stamp of a backyard through our kitchen window while washing dishes. Part of the dishwasher's duty was to collect crumbs for the birds. The dishwasher was an actual person. So the dishwasher had to put aside the bird crumbs so that Nana could feed them the next morning. Nana fed the birds religiously. We did a lot of things religiously. It only seemed right, since we went to parochial school. We went to church religiously; we took baths religiously; we cleaned our rooms on Saturday morning religiously; and we fed the birds religiously. The birds were never forgotten. This may seem like a small thing to feed the birds, but food was precious. We were never wasters. Nana and Mom claimed this as some core anthem of all those who survived The Depression. And I have rebelled against it ever since. I recycle and reuse, but I throw away the six peas left in the serving dish instead of putting them in a big plastic bag in the freezer to make vegetable soup one day with the carcass of a chicken I might cook in the future. I didn't even feed the birds breadcrumbs. My birds got store-bought bird seed. This did not stop Nana from collecting crusts after breakfast and throwing the crumbs onto my back lawn for our feathered friends. Luckily, I live in the woods, so I didn't have neighborhood watch complaining about the unsightly bread crusts dotting my otherwise pristine lawn. I didn't object to this manna-iacal practice of my grandmother; I just didn't do it. We watched the birds in the feeder, on the ground and in the bare trees.

The bird watching continued my childhood reverie. The girls would take turns washing dishes, and the dishwasher got to watch the bird revue. This was a very strict schedule between the four sisters as to whose turn it was to wash or dry the dishes or to be the busgirl and clear the table. Later, my stepfather would go on to say that we needed a lawyer to determine whose turn it was. (A subconscious will on my part to go to law school so I would never have to do the dishes?) At the time, I didn't realize the hidden benefit to the dishwashing job. Nana would be there to tell you if it was a cardinal, wren, blue jay, crow, or robin. This would translate itself into a much more complicated hobby with my husband who also loves bird watching. In my house, we also began to watch the birds from the kitchen dish-washing window when we were first married. My husband had worked hard to develop just the right bird feeders. A complicated affair to protect against squirrels poaching the precious birdseed. So as a married gal, I came to know the yellow-bellied sapsuckers and tufted titmouse. I would know that blue birds were rare and welcome visitors and blue jays were nasty warriors keeping all the other sweet little birds away from the food.

This day, Rachel climbed up on a chair to help wash the dishes. As she soaked herself with soapy water, Nana pointed out the various backyard visitors. Nana took special pride in the birds that ate her burnt toast as opposed to my laggards who only ate the store-bought seed.

This first blizzard day, we just bird watched and snow watched and kept the fire on a slow blaze. We stood at the kitchen window and washed dishes. We quietly felt the grace of an ordinary day. Let it snow, let it snow, let it snow.

DAY 63

Okay, it better stop the goddamn snowing. Cabin fever was a papal dispensation for swearing.

We played every game, watched every Barney episode, and cleaned everything. The cardinal had lost his charm. In fact, now he was a hazard, because it was time to fill the bird feeder. Those pig birds had eaten all the birdseed and ungraciously acted as if they deserved more. The female cardinal—you know the ugly brown thing with no pizzazz whatsoever—had the nerve to fly up against the window. I was certain she was saying, "Hey, where's the goddamn birdseed?" In my universe, birds were allowed to swear. But they were not allowed to demand waitress service in the middle of a blizzard.

The snow was about 13 inches deep now. As Nana said, "It's up to our giggy!"

Of course, my giggy had to go out and clear the paths and try and keep the driveway near the house clean so that my husband could eventually get home. Then, his giggy would have to work about four hours to clear the rest of the driveway. So much for peace, solitude and the wonders of nature.

As entertainment, we had taken eating to a new level. First we had breakfast. Then we baked cookies. Then with our cookies I offered coffee or juice, depending on age and how long I wanted each one awake. Then we had lunch. Then we decided what we would make for dinner and resumed baking a cake or pie for dessert. Thank God, snow shoveling burned a lot of calories. And in one of life's little jokes, Nana and Rachel seemed to be able to eat all they desired and it made not a whit of difference. Nana was not completely without vanity because she often commented with pride: "Look how skinny I am!" Great, now I had to look at People Magazine *and* my 92 year-old grandmother with envy.

At Christmastime in 1967, we had a blizzard in our small town. With well over twenty inches of snow, we were forbidden to go to Midnight Mass on Christmas Eve. We made a huge ruckus. I cried over this slight to the Baby Jesus and besides, it was a sin. We would all surely burn in hell for missing church on this most holy of days, Christmas. Oddly, any other Sunday we had no worry about the eternal fires of damnation. We battled to get out of going to Mass. All six of us just had to give my Mom and Nana a hard time. We didn't really want to go to midnight Mass on Christmas Eve. We just wanted to go out in the blizzard. Oh, and make sure Santa knew it wasn't OUR fault that we didn't go to church on Christmas.

Anyway, after Christmas Day was over, the snow just kept on coming. So to combat the claustrophobia, my Mom and Nana decided to teach us kids how to play Pinochle. It was remarkable. At that time my oldest sister was fifteen and my youngest brother was five. And truly, the only one who didn't learn how to play

Pinochle was my baby brother. We became quite good. We learned with one deck, with two decks, and how to play with a "kitty" when you only had three people instead of four. Most kids came back to school with a red bottom from sledding or spankings, or probably both. But the Hanover Street kids returned to school with something far more valuable: Pinochle skills.

So there we were, "fat, rag-ged and sassy" a favorite Nanaism, playing cards with a two-year-old. Not Pinochle of course, but UNO, where you could match colors and numbers. Of course, Nana helped Rachel, to the point where those two little card sharks would dance around the room and stick out their tongues at me when I lost.

DAY 65 (Nighttime)

Nana had taken to midnight trekking. She didn't leave the house. She just walked around doing things. She would use the bathroom. She wandered downstairs and made herself a cup of instant coffee. She would look for the newspaper and read yesterday's news. It didn't matter that it happened yesterday. She would become confounded to see that someone (she) had already completed the cryptoquote and the crossword puzzle. She got pissy about this because doing a crossword brought her such joy. Such a sense of accomplishment. That's when I would hear her whimpering. At first, I thought it was the dog dreaming. Then I realized, the dog doesn't turn on the lights. Rachel couldn't reach the light switch in the hallway. Since my husband was snoring contentedly next to me, I knew it wasn't his wandering I heard.

I've become a light sleeper—something I never was as a child or in college or even law school. In law school, I would curl up in a chair in the library and just fall asleep. I could "power nap" in the most comfy chairs in the library which were placed right in front of the elevator doors. It didn't matter how many times those hydraulics swooshed and clamored, I fell asleep. Motherhood robbed me of that talent. I heard everything now; real true uninterrupted sleep was a thing of the past. Maybe that was Nana's problem. She started mothering again at 62 years old, when we bounded into her row home demanding care and attention. Perhaps, she permanently lost the capacity for sleep. She was always waiting for the other shoe to drop. Is this our plight? No more real sleep, ever? Not even at 92 years old? I'll never make it.

I padded down to the kitchen.

"Nana, it's three o'clock in the morning. You should be sleeping."

"Is it, honey girl?"

"Yes, Nana, it really is. So come on, come back to bed."

"Who did the cryptoquote? You know I do the cryptoquote."

"Of course you do. You did it yesterday. You know I can't do those things. I don't have the patience."

"C'mon," I said. "Let's go upstairs. I'll get you the paper in the morning."

"Okay," she says.

Off we trudge. Hi ho hi ho.

I wondered how many times she did this with the six of us. I'm sure there were many a night where one of us was wandering the hallways of our childhood home. Actually, I was an occasional sleepwalker as a young child, so there's no way, I didn't wake her up on a night or two in my adolescent past. Since we were always underfoot in her house until we all got married or went to college, it never occurred to me that she was shepherding the troops of my brothers and sisters probably on a nightly basis.

The toddler started to cry.

"Oh crap," I murmured under my breath. "Not now, I am sooo tired."

"I know just how you feel," said Nana as she went into her room and firmly shut the door. Did she still feel that way when she heard a baby cry in the middle of the night?

DAY 67

Rachel had been croupy. So in my efforts to make everyone sleep at night, I put the baby gate at the top of the steps. That way Nana couldn't get downstairs. This was a disaster. Nana would not just give up and go back to bed. Why did I think she would? She never surrendered. She would work at that damn gate for fifteen minutes to try and figure out how to unlock it. I would listen to this finagling for thirteen minutes before jumping out of bed ready for battle.

"Nana! Let it go."

"But I can't get it open."

"Just where the hell are you going at 2 A.M.?"

"I couldn't find my watch."

"It's on your wrist."

"Oh, it must have got turned around so I couldn't read it."

"Please, just go back to bed."

"But I'm not tired."

"Well, I am, and I am not opening that gate. So just go to bed and read a magazine or something. Please, please, just go to bed."

"Okay, you don't have to get huffy about it. If I knew how to open that gate, I wouldn't have bothered you."

"Ugh, just--please--go--to--BED!"

My tirade woke up Rachel. God will always punish you for yelling at your grandmother.

DAY 68

As life usually does, today we went from the ridiculous to the sublime. Cindy needed further cancer treatment, but she was coming to an end of this round. She was positive and positively radiant since her hair was returning. The doctors suggested that she might want to consider prophylactic breast surgery and reconstruction as the form of her cancer is particularly virulent. She had the original reconstruction which had its ups and downs, but made her feel whole again. So this would mean revisiting that nightmare to hopefully prevent future nightmares.

You would think that this kind of news would be devastating. But in the three years that Cindy had been treating, she continued to look for answers in new places. Any hope to beat this bastard was hope and that did not bring her down but rather gave her focus to look for new directions and opportunities.

We tried to have this intense conversation over Saturday lunch.

"So what do you have to do?" I asked Cindy.

"They want me to consider having my right boob removed, even though there's no cancer there," she replied matter-of-factly.

"Why?"

"Well, apparently, the cancer in young pre-menopausal women is a raging bastard that just does not want to leave us alone, no matter what we do."

"An' Cinny?" Rachel asked.

"Yes, sweetie?"

"What's a bastard?"

"Eek!" I said and we looked at each other with wide eyes.

"It's a really mean person and a bad word, Rachey. Aunt Cindy made a boo-boo. So let's not say it anymore. Okay?"

"Okay, can I have your fench fies?"

"That's not what I think a bastard is," piped up Nana.

"Ooooo, Nana said a bad word," says Rachel, shaking her finger in Nana's face.

"What do you think it is?" Cindy said to Nana.

"Cindy, stop egging her on," I said.

"Honey girl, I am perfectly capable of talking for myself. A 'you-know-what'," she says looking sideways at Rachel, "is a child born out of wedlock."

"Nana?" said Rachel looking her directly in the eyes.

"Yes?"

"Can I have your fench fies?" Rachel says earnestly.

"Of course, honey girl."

"So, now that we've cleared that up," I said to Cindy, "what's your plan?"

"I don't know. I have to talk to some other doctors, and I have to finish this round of chemo. Then I can decide. I wonder how you pick out a new 'rack'?" she said.

"Cindy, if this can help and the surgery is not all that risky, I think you should do it," I told her.

"I know," she said with tears in her eyes, "but I'm so tired of all of it. I just want to go to work, go home, go out and have fun and live an ordinary life. I would love an ordinary life. I would revel in it. I would never ask for more. I don't think I ever have actually."

The tears spilled down both of our faces. We tried to hide them from our lunch companions. They were too busy fighting over a happy ending sundae to pay attention to our boring medical conversation.

"Look, at least you'll get the breasts you always dreamed of," I told her.

"I think Larry is looking forward to that. It beats all the puking and the baldness," she said with a laugh as we both wipe our tears with napkins.

"Daddy bald," said Rachel.

We left the restaurant and spent the afternoon in the mall of terror from weeks ago, with an eagle eye on Nana at all times. It was a lot easier with another adult to help me. I think the companionship of these two gave Cindy something else to think about. My heart and my breasts ached for her, but I was helpless. The beauty of an ordinary day should never be lost on any bastard.

DAY 69

"God please forgive me for counting the days until Nana goes home. I should know that this is her home. I should be grateful that I can return the favor. But it's so damn hard. Now, I should shut up and stop whining like a baby. Amen."

If I ever wondered why I chose to be a lawyer and not a nurse like my mother, today I realized it in spades. Nana hadn't been feeling well. She seemed listless and out of sorts. I took her to the doctor. Her vitals seemed to check out, but the doctor thought some tests should be run. They took blood and sent us home to await the results. Oh yeah, and while we are at home we should get a urine sample and bring it back in for testing.

"A what?" I tried to say calmly.

"A urine sample," the Doctor said calmly. Of course she was calm. She had no idea what this might entail (pardon the pun). I had no idea what this might entail.

"Look," she said, "it's really very simple. Just have her pee into this cup and that's it."

"Fine," I said not convinced that "that's it."

I decided to do this after lunch. On the other hand, I might lose my cookies. No, definitely lunch first, it would delay the inevitable.

At lunch, we talked about our old house on Hanover Street. I hate to drive by there with Nana in the car because I know how much she missed it. In the *ironies of life* category, she got screwed on this one.

My grandmother had basically tricked my grandfather into buying this house. They had been renters for many years. My grandfather was certain that they could never afford a house, but Nana was much wiser. Despite the call of the drink, my grandfather worked steadily throughout his life. They both did. So Nana just believed that they could have a house, and she was bound and determined to get one.

As the story goes, she put a down payment on the $8,000 house, and then told Pop-Pop she bought it. Her children were teenagers by then, and the house they were living in along the railroad tracks was to be torn down. In her effort to find affordable housing, Nana decided they could afford to buy a house. So she did it. Pop-Pop was said to be furious, but they completely owned that house in a very short period of time. By the way, my family doesn't come from the right or wrong side of the tracks. We come *from* the tracks.

As to the irony, my mother and grandmother decided that my mom should own the house on Hanover Street that Nana worked so hard to possess. That way, if anything happened to Nana, my mom and the kids would have a roof over their heads. So Nana transferred the house to Mom. Thirteen years later my mom got remarried, Nana moved in with Mom and eventually Nana's beloved little house that was the imprimatur of her independence was sold. So Nana, even in the best of health, could never go back. In this small town we have to pass that house almost every place we go, and we always stare and sigh.

That's what we talked about over lunch. The joys of Hanover Street. How Mom and Nana cemented over the backyard, because we kids were forever ripping up the lawn. The backyard was probably 8'x10'. We went from grass stains to skinned knees. Really? That was your decision? We can't take care of the grass...the kids, oh they'll be fine on the cement.

Our matriarchs were wise enough to build two cement "planters" along the edges of the backyard so that they could still have a bit of nature around them. Somehow, Nana managed to keep at least ten beautiful rose plants on the perimeter of the cement. My favorites were the tea roses. The rose bushes were impressionist beauty in the cement pond. They were orange, yellow, pink and cream all in the same flower. Tea roses made me think maybe we were people who "had tea." At least we had tea roses. But as wise children who learned from years of experience, we stayed away from the beauty along our playground. To fall into a rose bush once would cure you of that mistake forever. When I look back on it, I am pretty amazed that six kids in one house found an 8'x10' square of cement to be the ideal playground. We would spend hours out there, playing tag, catching lightning bugs, "sleeping out," drawing hopscotch and four square plans on the concrete with chalk, and caricatures of teachers or neighbors (and then pray for rain so the neighborhood bully wouldn't recognize himself—or be able to read his name in big, huge letters next to his big huge head).

And even if the concrete was off limits for the day, because there were eight lines of laundry out there on the most beautiful days of the week, creativity in play did not escape six children. I looked at Nana and asked her if she knew how we used to throw things out the third floor window to see if we could hit the hedge below.

"What kind of things?" she wanted to know.

"Oh, you know—books, scarves, stuffed animals. C'mon, you know we used to do that don't you?"

I'm sure we must've gotten into trouble for this. We got into trouble for so many antics that I can't remember all the punishments.

"No, I don't think so. But I do remember finding things in the hedge and wondering what kind of crazy game you kids were playing."

"But you never said anything?"

"Oh for heaven's sake, honey girl, you were kids. Sometimes it's best to just let things go."

Speaking of letting things go. Sigh. The urine sample.

We went to the bathroom, and I explained the process.

"It's really very simple; just hold this cup under you, and pee into it. Okay?"

"What?"

"Nana, just do it."

"Why?"

"So the doctor can see why you don't feel well."

"But, I feel fine."

"No, you don't."

"Yes, I do."

"No, you really don't. Now pee into the cup. Okay?"

"But..."

"Nana, if you don't pee into the cup, I'm going to have to kill you."

"Oh piddle."

"Yes, exactly; now just do it, for God's sake."

"You don't have to swear."

"Nana!"

"Oh, alright."

She couldn't do it. She couldn't keep herself and the cup balanced. We tried again. She missed the cup completely. I went downstairs and retrieved a can from the recycling and peed into it, so I could show her what to do. It didn't matter. She just didn't get it. We began laughing. Hysterics took over. The upside was, it was easy to pee when you were laughing. The downside was you still couldn't hold the cup steady. And then yes, I did the unthinkable; I held the cup while she peed into it. A bitter success. I washed my hands forty-three times throughout the rest of the day. Rachel closely observed these antics like she was viewing a scientific experiment. She took it all in. I hoped she would store this in her memory banks so she'll know what to do when I'm 92.

DAY 70

I couldn't even believe how tired one human being can be.

But in the heat of maniacal behavior, one reality check that hit home to me was this: I was the only one yelling. My husband almost never raised his voice except to call me from the garage when he was hanging precariously from a ladder.

I was trying to create self-rescue through the use of the raised voice. I thought that if I were loud enough, everyone would do what they were supposed to do, and I would be relieved from whatever it was that was bothering me at the moment. The problem with that was that I didn't always know what was bothering me at the moment. I didn't have time to reflect upon whether or not my noxious reaction to the situation was founded in fantasy or exhaustion or reality.

Nana and Rachel called me on things all the time. Nana wouldn't hesitate to point out that I was in a tizzy for no reason.

"Honey girl, what is all the fuss about?"

"I just want to get this place cleaned up, for crying out loud!" I would say to no one in particular, actually.

"Well, then, let's just clean it up. Getting all cranky about it, isn't going to get the job done, now is it?"

Ugh, I hated when she was right.

So I had to formulate some kind of a plan to breathe or count to ten, or do a quick crazy yoga stretch. But this all went back to how tired I was. I couldn't stop being tired because I couldn't stop being on guard. I had to be on watch incessantly, endlessly and ceaselessly—even when I was sleeping. I was the keeper of safety and light. I guided the way and kept all harm from the door. This was not constant conscious thought; this was just the ever vigilant energy required to take care of people you love.

DAY 71

Nana accused me of stealing her teeth.

What, pray tell would I do with these teeth? Now Rachel could have actually used the teeth since she was pretty low in that commodity. But I hadn't seen her with them, and I doubted that she would understand the installation process.

What could Nana have done with her teeth? The answer was *"anything."* Yes, she could have thrown them away. She could have put them in the freezer. She could have put them in the dog's dish. She could have given them to the dog as a gift. She's a very generous person.

We began the search and rescue of the errant false teeth. The whole time we were looking for the teeth, Nana was gumming her distaste for the pursuit.

"I dimdn't do it."

"I'm sure it was inadvertent, Nana."

"Der mot im my cump."

"What?"

"My cump. Der not dar."

"My cump? My cump? What in the hell is your goddamn cump?"

She holds up a pink plastic container in the shape of a large three-dimensional diaphragm holder.

"Oh, your CUP. The cup you clean your teeth in. Okay, good. We know your teeth aren't in there."

"What mid see do mid dem?"

"Who?"

Alarmingly, I totally understood what Nana was saying without her teeth. She wanted to know: "What did she do with them?"

"Her," Nana said and pointed to Rachel.

Rachel started to snivel. She didn't like being fingered. She knew she was being accused.

I picked Rachel up and tried to console her. I also took a glimpse of her mouth and hands to see if she was hiding the offending teeth. She was not, and she was offended. She screamed louder.

"Okay, honey. It's okay. Let's put in a tape."

She pushed her way out of my arms and ran to the TV. Her real comforter. Quite frankly, that was good enough for me. I had teeth to find. Let Big Bird and Elmo take care of the situation with Rachel.

"Nana, what do you usually do with your teeth when you go to bed?"

"My cump."

"Right. So, do you remember going to bed last night?"

"Mhm."

"Let's start there."

We went into her bedroom. Surprisingly, everything looked normal. Nothing in any crazy places.

I looked on the dresser. No teeth. I looked on her bedside table. No teeth. I looked on the floor, under the bed, in the closet.

She made her bed diligently and immaculately every morning. I saw no teeth chomping to get out through the covers.

I sat on the bed in frustration. I threw my head back on the pillow. The hard, crunchy pillow. Slowly, I lifted the pillow. There they were, as cruddy as that place behind the refrigerator that no one has seen for years.

"Oh my God, Nana, these are disgusting!"

"What?"

She grabbed the teeth from under the pillow and tried to put them in her mouth.

"Noooo!"

I practically put her in a chokehold to get the teeth before she could put them in.

"They have to be cleaned—immediately," I said.

For about six months, I thought to myself.

I gingerly placed the teeth between my fingers. I found her cump, but that too needed nuclear blasting.

I took the box of Efferdent, the unopened box—have I not been paying attention? I went downstairs with the offending teeth.

"I'm sorry, Nana but I just have to get these teeth clean first."

"Dat's okay," she said and trundled off to watch Bert and Ernie.

Charlie Chaplin said that life is tragic up close, but from far away it is hysterical. I wished I were far away. I saw the humor here…after all a good cump story was funny, right? It made for great cocktail party conversation—like I'd been to a cocktail party.

They finished Sesame Street and looked for lunch. I needed to make sure the offending false teeth were clean, so I turned lunch into a game of soft food with no teeth required. The teeth had to soak, at least through nap time. I was wondering if I could microwave false teeth. I considered looking that up on the internet while they were sleeping.

"Let's have applesauce and ice cream for lunch!"

"Yayyy", said Rachel.

"I don't want applesauce," barked the toothless one.

Actually, what she said was, "I dn wn appasas".

"Okay, how about just ice cream?"

"Yayyyy!!"

"Too cold." Nana snapped back. "Where's my teeth?"

"What would you like for lunch, Nana?"

"Oh, I don know, anyfing ull do."

Luckily, I am holding an ice cream scoop and not a butcher knife.

"Okay then, oatmeal for Nana and ice cream for Rachel and Mommy."

"Yayyy!"

By the way, you can—and I did—microwave false teeth.

DAY 72

Even though I couldn't accomplish much during the day, we couldn't really relax or sit still. The two of them had to be entertained. We engaged in a barrage of games, songs, dancing, eating, bathing, and cleaning, cleaning, cleaning. You'd think my house would have been immaculate. But you would be mistaken. Because we didn't truly clean to military standards. We just acted like we were cleaning. At least I did. The other two thought they really were engaging in helpful activity. If I handed them a rag that smelled like Pine-sol or a can of Pledge and a dust cloth and set them free, the house smelled great, and I could pay a bill, wash a dish or go pee in peace.

When my husband came home from work, the two of them were falling over each other to brag about their accomplishments of the day.

"Look Daddy, I keen it!" squealed Rachel.

"That's right, honey girl," chimed in Nana, "we worked all day so that Mommy could have a rest."

Why did that make me want to kill her? So, what if she wants a little credit, a little attention, especially from the man of the house.

This also made me want to kill her.

I love my husband. But this adoration by my grandmother made me nuts. I didn't think it was jealousy. I did think it was sort of prodigal-son-ish. I was with her all day long; I took care of her every need; I kept her safe and entertained. And my husband got the goodies. When he came home, or if he was working out in the garden, all activities ceased to bring him sustenance. If we were serving a meal, he was always served first. A plate would be removed from someone by Nana if it had not gone to the man first, and given over to the man at the table.

I first noticed this when I was just out of law school and working at a small firm just down the street from my mother's house. I would stop in almost every day to have lunch with Nana. This gave my mother a little break. Truthfully, I loved these lunches. Nana was in complete control of her faculties, and we had a great time. We would discuss current events.

"What exactly is the Quaaaaaalude?" Nana asked one day, with her unique pronunciation, as she read in the newspaper about one of her favorite local doctors who was arrested for manufacturing the drug.

"'Ludes, Nana, just call them that. And they're bad."

"I don't believe it. I'm sure he was just trying to help people."

"He certainly was," I said, "he was trying to help the local drug dealers do a better business. He's a great community leader."

"Oh, hush up, you bold thing."

We would discuss the latest cryptoquote. We might commiserate about my mother's lot in life. Since Nana was now living with my mother and stepfather, she had an inside view into my Mom's own ups and downs. Basically, Nana and I would gossip about family and friends. It was great.

Not long after these lunches began, my sister Cindy would come with her boyfriend. And not long after that, my baby sister, Caren, would come with her baby. We were not always together so this is when I discovered the pecking order.

If Cindy's boyfriend was there before me, or we sat down together, he would always be served first. It did not matter who had to get back to work, or who had time to kill, the man was served first. If the man came after all the women were seated, a plate of food was taken from any unsuspecting woman and moved to the man's place.

There was even a pecking order for women. Because I was a *working* woman, I would get served first, if no men were present. The fact that I had a job just raised my status above my sister with the baby. Women can be their own worst enemies, even today.

So the pecking order never changes.

DAY 74

A vacation. Someone had come to rescue me. My sisters realized that keeping Nana was not a dream job. They chipped in to send me on a bed and breakfast weekend for my birthday. My husband and I got in the car and drove for hours and hours with no car seat, no Cheerios, no Depends. It was a dream.

Cindy moved into my house for the weekend. I worried that chemotherapy would look fun after spending 24/7 with these two.

My husband and I acted like grown-ups for about five minutes. Then we acted like children.

We went outside and played in the snow. We got wet and silly and tired and hungry. Unfortunately, the bed and breakfast was literally in the middle of nowhere. There was nothing to do, no place to go for dinner. It was a challenge for my husband. He was just not the kind of guy to sit around and do nothing for three days. One day, maybe. So we got creative. We took long walks along the canal. We drove more hours and hours looking for food, shopping and hole-in-the-wall entertainment. Secretly, my husband was glad to have some undivided attention from his wife. Secretly, his wife was glad to be taken care of and have nothing to do, no decisions to make, and no one looking at her for guidance.

The bare trees of winter somehow looked better here. The food tasted better. The sheets seemed crisper, more comforting. The sun shined brighter, and the air was cleaner. None of that was really true, but I was just so *free*. I would have been just as content to sit on that bed and read a book for three days—uninterrupted. That was the gift—Mommy, uninterrupted.

It was a glorious weekend. I was refreshed. I was a girl who married a great guy and that was all that mattered. We told stupid jokes, we ate naughty food, and we did naughty things. We liked each other and our life together. We got back into the car for the long, lazy drive home and I realized :

Oh crap, it's over.

DAY 78

I returned. No one really noticed. Everyone was happy while we were gone, and I suppose I should have been grateful for that. But as my husband and I walked into the house, Rachel was busy with crayons and paper, and Nana and Cindy were having tea.

"We're home!"

"Well, hello honey girl," said Nana.

"Hey Rachey, Mommy and Daddy are home!"

I saw Rachel in the family room with her head down over her paper and diligently coloring. Without looking up she said:

"This is important. I have to go to work."

I had no idea where that came from, but I saw a CEO in my future.

We exchanged weekend information, and Cindy took her leave. She survived quite nicely, thank you very much. I was hopeful that that meant she would return for another dose of caregiving in the future.

We all settled back into our routines, and the vacation was just enough to convince me that I would make it through the next four months.

As nighttime fell, Nana went to bed without a hitch, as did Rachel. With everyone snug in their beds, I settled down with my book, the fireplace crackling, and quiet humming all around me. Blessed peace. I guessed we all needed a break from each other. An hour after everyone was in bed, and surely well asleep I thought, I heard Nana rattling around in her bedroom upstairs. She came down with a box of Whitman's Sampler in her hand.

"Anyone want a piece of candy?" she asked.

DAY 79

Nana, like many women her age, had become so attached to her pocketbook that whole continents might erupt into global war if one attempted to relieve her of this prized possession.

The pocketbook seemed to have become the symbol of the last vestige of independence and possession. This small, or rather large by pocketbook standards, symbol of ownership carried women of Nana's generation through their day with confidence. I defy you to go to any personal care facility, assisted living, nursing home or even mother-in-law apartment and find a woman NOT in possession of her beloved pocketbook. If they are in possession of their pocketbooks, they are in possession of their world. They may no longer have their home, car, furniture or spouse, but they have their pocketbook, damn it, and they will be the sovereign of this kingdom until the day they die. I believe we should place these last repositories of "stuff" with our loved ones in their caskets. These women look naked without their purse. To have them clutching the one item that has not forsaken them would give them a final look of triumph over the material world.

However, this pocketbook obsession for the living can cause problems.

"C'mon, Nana, I just want to run to the store for some milk."

"I need my pocketbook."

"No you don't. I have money, and we'll be right back."

"I can't go without my pocketbook."

"Really, Nana, it's okay. We're coming right back."

What was I doing? I knew how important this purse was to her. It was *literally* everything to her. Every possible thing that she could control was in that pocketbook. And each day she wanted to know that somewhere, somehow, she was is in control of something.

"Okay, let's look."

First, we looked in the obvious places.

"Is it in your bedroom?" Up the stairs we went to her bedroom. We looked under the bed, in the closet, in her drawers, and on the bookshelf. Nope. We moved to the bathroom. A cursory look in the tiny bathroom revealed no such thing as a pocketbook. I did surreptitiously put an Efferdent tablet in her 'cump' for cleaning as she started down the stairs for the next reconnaissance.

"How about the dining room?" I asked her.

"Honey girl, why would I put my pocketbook in the dining room?"

I don't know. Why would you wander around at 3 A.M.? with box of Whitman's Samplers? Is the dining room so crazy a notion?

"Let's look anyway."

We trudged through the dining room, the living room, the coat closet, the hallway and ended up in the family room. That produced no pocketbook, but plenty of dirty glasses, used tissues and an old pretzel.

"Well, Nana, you got any other ideas?" I asked her.

"Hmmmm," she said.

"Mommy…"

"Yes, Rachel?"

"I find Nana's pottyboot," she said so adorably.

"Ok, baby, you can look too," I said. By this time I forgot where we were going and why we even needed to go there.

"No, Mommy, I *find* it," she said with authority.

"Really? Where is it?" I replied, totally not believing her.

She walked into the laundry room. Nana and I followed her, and Rachel pointed to the pocketbook, sitting on the floor behind all the snow boots.

And just what was in this pocketbook? A few tissues, some used, her insurance cards, her Social Security card from 1954, family pictures, a few dollars and some change in a small change purse, some hard tac (candy),a lipstick, in a racy shade of red-orange which she did indeed wear much to my chagrin, and a comb the size of a loaf of bread.

DAY 80

Time to take the girls to the doctor. Rachel seemed to be harboring an ear infection; Nana was remarkably listless. She probably needed blood work. This was how the conversation went with the Nurse Practitioner:

Me: Nana seems listless.

Nurse: Well, she is 92.

Me: Yes, I know that, but she isn't herself.

Nurse: In what way?

Me: She's listless.

Nurse: For an old lady?

Me: Please don't say that; it offends her.

Nana: I am sitting right here, honey girl.

Me: Yes, Nana, I know. I'm sorry.

Nurse: What would you like me to do?

Me: Gee, I don't know. How about some blood work?

Nurse: I guess I could do that.

Me: Is that okay with you, Nana?

Nana: Whatever you say, honey girl.

Me (to Nurse Nutcase): Do you think you could take her blood pressure now?

Nurse: I guess so.

Me (to Nana): The Nurse is going to take your blood pressure, and then we'll go get some blood work done, okay?

Nurse: "Nurse PRACTITIONER"

Imagine that. Nana's blood pressure was dangerously low, and she also needed a blood transfusion. Yes, because she has suffered from serious anemia and diverticulitis and lots of other crap over her 92 years, she needed her "cocktail" of blood. Now some would think this is a waste on a 92-year-old, but since the last time she had a blood boost, my bathroom had never been so clean, my laundry never folded so well and my toddler and my Labrador never so entertained, so who should judge the quality of life here?

Nurse PRACTITIONER also treated Rachel on the same day.

Nurse: So what seems to be the problem?

Me: She's not herself.

Nurse: In what way?

Me: She's listless. I think she has an ear infection.

Nurse: Why would you think that?

Me: Because I'm her mother.

Nurse: Does she have a fever?

Me: No.

Nurse: Does she have a rash?

Me: No.

Nurse: Is she pulling at her ear?

Me: No.

Nurse (Snorting): Well, then what makes you think it's an ear infection?

Me: Well, let me see, every time she gets an ear infection, she's listless. She never spikes a fever until the infection is well on its way, and her symptoms are never classic. But nine times out of ten, it's an ear infection and I come back about three days later and it's in both ears. That's what makes me think it's an ear infection.

Nurse: Well, let's just see.

She retrieved the otoscope. Looked in one ear.

Nurse: Hmm.

Nurse PRACTITIONER looked in the other ear.

Nurse: Yep.

Me: Well?

Nurse: Double ear infections.

I don't know why this made me jubilant. I wanted to run around the office like Rocky with my arms raised in victory. Then I realized my prize was a crabby kid with an ear infection and a grandmother with blood running like water. But still I did nail it, after all.

MOM PRACTITIONER!!!

DAY 81

We were taking Nana to the hospital the next day for a few days so that she could have her blood transfusion. Meanwhile she needed rest. Nana hadn't rested in 92 years; she didn't know how to rest. She started her working career as a young girl cleaning other people's houses. Then she worked in the farmer's market, then waitressing and cleaning local businesses. Those endless menial jobs continued as long as she could do them which I don't think would have ever ended if she hadn't had to help her daughter. And in her blessed old age, here we came, her six grandchildren, and she had to work again. God, how did she never complain? Never.

I think about how my girlfriends and I complained about our children, our husbands, and our "problems." Should we work? Should we have another baby? Should we spend money on a massage? We didn't even know what problems were. And I never once heard my Mom and Nana sit around complaining about us or about how hard their life was. Maybe they were so busy, they didn't have time? I don't think so. I think they really didn't believe it was a bad life. They kept a roof over our heads (not even their heads, our heads) and clothes on our back and food on our table and that was enough. That was great, in fact. They knew what it was like to be hungry, to be worried about having work. To be able to stay at home and actually take care of the children without the need for another job outside the home was a luxury. To complain about that would be heresy.

Truth be told, having two mothers was great. Truth be told by them, each of those mothers having a "wife" to pick up the slack was not so bad either. I'm sure my brothers would have liked a man's influence, but whatever it was they learned at the hands of six women, made them chick magnets for the rest of their lives. Not a bad deal.

So Nana's incessant need for "work" had made me a creative employer. I tried to trick Nana into resting by coming up with seated chores like folding the laundry. This worked for awhile until she ran out of laundry. She was a machine. I couldn't keep up with her. And it was not just folding. It was crisp lines, fluted sleeves, and thwack with the towels. I was running the washing machine like a hotel laundry just to keep Nana busy. I resorted to washing beach towels in March, tablecloths that haven't been used since the Nixon resignation, and some thongy things I found in the bottom of my underwear drawer. These last items didn't need folding and I had to explain what in God's name the stringy things were for, but as long as they were washed, and needed to be folded, they served a purpose.

I convinced my washerwoman to lie down with Rachel for a nap. They had become pretty good nap buddies. I put them both in the queen-size bed in the guestroom. Nana would read a book or two, sometimes Rachel corrected her interpretation of "Ernie Takes a Bath", and they would eventually fall asleep. Snoring could be a blessing from heaven if you looked at it the right way.

I spent the next two hours putting away the clean laundry and shoving the thongy things back in the bottom drawer in case my husband got any crazy ideas that this was preparation and not desperation.

There did seem to be an upside of gargantuan morning chores followed by a nap. Nana seemed to slow down just a bit. She agreed to 'babysit' while I ran the vacuum, started dinner and ran outside to feed the birds. She was resting, but I had to give it a "work" name so that all respectability remained intact.

DAY 82

Nana was required to stay in the hospital for a day or two in order to assess the effectiveness of the blood transfusion. God forgive me, but I also was happy for the break. I knew she would be taken care of for those two days. It felt like a vacation, a vacation that did not last two hours, because Nana was not a very good patient.

"I don't like this thing," Nana looked at me with disdain.

"What thing?"

"This rag they want me to wear."

"Nana, they want you to wear the hospital gown because the blood transfusion might get messy and they don't want to ruin your own pretty nightgown."

"It's ugly."

Who the hell did she think was looking at her couture?

"And it's as thin as a wafer. How am I supposed to be comfortable in this?"

She had a point. Hospital gowns are ugly and uncomfortable. And since she had no circulation to begin with, she'd probably freeze to death before the transfusion kicked in.

"Let me see what I can do."

At the nurses' desk, I expected to meet with resistance. I didn't meet with anyone. Anywhere. Ever, apparently.

"Hello? Helloooo?"

"Can I help you?" A nurse appeared out of nowhere.

"Yes, my grandmother is here for a blood transfusion..."

"Oh, that would be Janine's patient."

"Yes, but Janine doesn't seem to be around right now..."

"I'm sure she'll be right back."

The phone rings, and Nurse Helpful answered it. I was dismissed.

I went around the corner and spied a room full of hospital gowns in all colors. The brighter the color, the more she would like it. (Please see Day 28 re: orange brocade coat)

I picked out three brightly colored gowns and a couple of flannel blankets and took the contraband back to Nana. Nana was standing next to her bed. She put her orange brocade coat back on over her hospital gown. She was holding her pocketbook tightly in anticipation of escape.

"No dice, Nana."

"What, honey girl?"

"Look at these nice fresh p.j.'s I've brought you. And some warm blankets. Let's go. You have to get changed."

"I don't like it here."

"Who does? It's a hospital. But you need the blood to feel better."

"Okay," Nana said with remarkable compliance.

I helped her change out of her coat and got her comfortable. I explained the phone and the TV. She would have no independent recollection of these instructions, I knew. I turned on the TV and chose a program she liked. Nurse Janine arrived.

"How are we?"

"We're just fine. When will you set up the transfusion?"

"Well, let me see here. Margaret is it?"

Nana just nodded her head.

"The doctor should be here any time now, and we can get started. It should only take a few hours and then you can go home."

"WHAT? Sorry, Nan. Excuse me, Janine, but the doctor said she would have to stay for at least a day or two."

"Oh, I doubt that. What do the doctors know anyway? The insurance probably wouldn't pay for an overnight. As long as everything goes okay. So you just stop by in about two or three hours and we'll see how she's doing. Make sure you leave your number at the desk."

I kissed Nana goodbye.

"It's going to be fine, Nana. You'll feel so much better, you'll have to start spring cleaning a month early."

"Okay, honey girl. I'm going to take a nap now."

"You do that, I'll be back after lunch."

I will forever remember lunch that day as one of the calmest hours of my life. With Rachel at the sitter and Nana safely ensconced in the hospital, I had a lunch of my own. All alone. With an actual newspaper. I was horrified to find that the world was in a mess. But I savored each word as a morsel of intelligent life melting over my tongue like the Belgian chocolate of enlightenment.

My cell phone rang. The hospital. She couldn't be done already. It had only been an hour. There wasn't time to even get the blood into her. Oh my God! Something terrible had happened.

"Hello?"

"Mrs. Sikorski?"

"Yes, what? Is she alright?"

"I'm calling about your grandmother."

"Yes, I know. Is she alright?"

"She's fine. But she'll be here a bit longer than we expected."

"Well, what's wrong with her?" I asked, very calmly.

"She pulled the IV tube out, tried to get out of bed, and there's blood everywhere."

"Holy crap! Uh, sorry. I mean, Oh my goodness."

It was really very, very hard not to start laughing.

"I'm so sorry," I said, "she's really not violent or anything. I can't imagine why she would do that."

"Well in any event, she will have to be strapped down now."

"Oh my God, No! Don't do that. I'll be right there."

That newspaper had nothing on me in the disaster department.

I returned to find Nana strapped down and crying.

I tried my damnedest to remove the restraints while restraining myself from hospital genocide.

"Oh Nana, for heaven's sake. What were you thinking?"

"I don't know, honey girl. I just wanted to go home."

"Sweetie, we are going home. In a few hours, maybe tomorrow. But you have to behave yourself. I only left for lunch. I was coming right back."

Now I was crying.

"I'm sorry, Nana. Were you scared?"

"Oh, of course not, I just didn't like it here. They're nasty, and it smells."

"Nana--"

"I know honey girl, I'm sorry."

"I will stay for a while, if you behave, maybe I can get these restraints off right now, but I need to get help to do it. I'll be right back."

"Okay, honey girl."

Back to the nurses' station.

"Look, you need to take the restraints off my grandmother."

"I'm sorry, but she is a danger to herself and others."

I was exercising great restraint here myself.

"She's fine. She just wanted to go home. But she promises to be a good patient. I will stay for a few hours, and she'll be fine. I promise."

"I'm sorry."

"So am I. I need your supervisor right now."

And so it went. I conversed politely with the supervisor, with the head of nurses, and finally not so politely with Nana's doctor. What a shock, the doctor saw it my way. I stayed with her until late at night when the transfusion was over and she had fallen into a deep sleep. Nana behaved from then on until I could get there. When I came to pick her up, she couldn't be perkier. Even though the benefits were far reaching, I hoped we never would have to go back to those bastards.

DAY 83

I was potty training and retraining. Rachel would tell me when she had to go. Nana would tell me after she had an accident. This required critical thinking to devise a plan of action for both parties. They were also picking up on each other's foibles. Rachel figured that if Nana could wait to tell, so could she. What was good for the goose was good for the gander. This philosophy would return to haunt me many times I feared.

Nana didn't like Depends. They had not yet devised good Depends. These were bulky with straps like our old sanitary napkins. God, how I hated those things. They felt like horrendous chastity belts. Perhaps that was the point. If you weren't comfortable down there, maybe you wouldn't let anyone else there either. Now young girls wear thongs all the time. Yet, if we told them to strap on a sanitary napkin they would be horrified. I got news for them; it's the same damn thing as a thong. But, I digress. Depends at Nana's age felt humiliatingly like diapers. Who likes diapers?

Actually, Rachel did; she loved them. She saw no reason to advance to big girl panties. Diapers made her life easy. I knew, as all mothers knew, that she would be in high school and not potty trained. Of course, then when she's ninety, she'd feel right at home.

Nana resented the Depends, and I didn't blame her. So I tried to give her a break and let her wear normal underwear. I was watching her like I watched Rachel. Every hour or two, I would ask both of them:

"Do you have to go potty, Rachel?"

"No."

"Nana?"

"What?"

"Do you have to go potty, I mean do you have to go to the bathroom?"

I was trying to maintain everyone's dignity around here, but it eroded with time.

"No," Nana would say to me.

Why did I trust them? Nothing in the past three months had given me any reason to trust either one of them.

"Oh, dear."

"What Nana?"

" I beshit myself."

"You what?"

"I beshit myself."

She seemed to believe that using the Shakespearian term for what she had just done, somehow gave her authority and the right to have avoided going to the bathroom in the first place. Like it's your fault that she had done this unthinkable thing, and if couched most pleasantly in good tongue, you would realize the error of your ways, and fix this most unpleasant problem posthaste.

"Mommy?"

"Not now, honey, I have to help Nana."

"Okay, but I beshit myself too."

Rachel's interpretation of this phrase was exactly on point as we say in the law.

I could only change one diaper at a time. Luckily, Rachel was content to sit there and wait her turn. I wondered if this is what twins feel like. No, because, I could whip off a diaper in public with my child. I could reprimand her if necessary, and everyone would think that was fine. But I could not do the same with my grandmother. I shouldn't even be allowed to do the same with her. This was the challenge. I wanted to treat her like a two-year-old child. I wanted to yell at her for misbehaving or throw caution to the wind when it's time to change the Depends. It was difficult to remember that she was an adult—an adult who raised me with tender loving care; an adult who was in charge, had ideas, was independent and looked to for advice and consent.

It's hard to remember, when the jelly was coursing down her sweater and she didn't see it, that she wiped my face, and my behind. Or when she did "beshit" herself and wouldn't acknowledge that, it's hard to remember not to yell that she should get herself to the bathroom. Why couldn't she remember to do that? I made allowances for the child, but if I made allowances for the adult then I began to think that I had the right to treat her like a child. This was not a thought process; it was just a reaction. It was the way we dealt with each other. The thought process came when I was lying in bed remembering if I had done the wrong thing. I treated the adult in a disrespectful way. I know this because I made her cry. Somehow that hurts more than when your baby cries. That's when the bell tolls, and I know it would one day toll for thee.

DAY 85

Old people have turned their clocks back to baby time. They often go to bed very early especially in the winter. Somehow darkness beckons them to rest. I'm not sure if this is because they are still the generation of farmers and Depression workers who worked from dawn to dusk and were grateful for the permission of sundown to rest and sleep, or if it's because there just isn't that much to do after dusk. With darkness, there is no place to go or anything to do. Television required too much or too little of Nana's concentration, and reading could only be done for an hour perhaps. Then she was just too tired to pursue any further activity.

But the reverse of this was that if she went to bed a bit after sundown, then she was likely to awaken before sunrise. That's when the bride of Frankenstein appeared. She would wander around the house in search of a mission. Sometimes the paper boy had not yet arrived with a newspaper to entertain her. *Note*: As you know, my driveway is 787- feet long. My paper is not delivered to my front door. In order to read the paper, you must walk 787 feet to retrieve it, and another 787 feet to get back. And you must do this all in the dark, and with the dog, because, *like idiots*, we trained him to go with us in the morning for his constitutional. We didn't know that five years later, he would have to be in charge of an old lady.

Although the newspaper is by far her most coveted form of entertainment, we would not allow Nana to make the 787-foot trek. We had to devise ways to prevent her from being the Sherpa of the day. Mostly, my husband would get up at 5:30 AM to get out the door before she awakened. Then, when she came downstairs, the coffee would be made and the paper would be on the counter waiting for her. It was a pretty classy hotel.

On occasion, I would hear my husband run to the bottom of the steps in the dark of the morning to stop Nana from going out the front door. Oh, and there were three very large dogs who lived at the end of our driveway, who liked to follow whoever went out for the paper back up the driveway to our door for a snack. And one little teensy thing more: The dogs barked the entire time the paper retriever was out there thus waking the entire neighborhood. Sleep deprivation was shared among the neighbors.

If we were lucky enough to survive the newspaper debacle, we could then tiptoe around saying, "SHH" as loudly as possible so that we wouldn't wake the toddler. This was very important on mornings where the toddler had been up in the middle of the night for one of the myriad reasons toddlers don't want to sleep during nocturnal hours.

Generally, there were three to five sleep deprived nights per week. We were not happy, and often we were stupid. We would forget the diaper bag, or to pay bills, or to bring the checkbook to the grocery store. We would get snippy with the lawn guy and hostile with the telemarketer.

Telemarketers should have an asterisk next to the young mothers who have not yet caught up on their sleep and avoid these households at all costs.

"Hello."

"Hello, may I please speak to Mrs. Skskersky?"

"Who? Oh, never mind, what can I help you with?"

"Mrs. Skskersksyskys?"

"Yes, whatever. What is it?"

"How are you today, ma'am?"

"How am I? How am I? I'll tell you how I am. I haven't slept in eight days. I haven't actually slept in three years, what with being pregnant and all. I am tired. That's how I am. I am so goddamn tired, I can hardly see straight. I don't know what day it is, what time it is, or why I actually came into this room. I just want to go lie down and wake up ten years from now. That's how I am. Now just what the hell do you want?"

"Hello? Hello?"

DAY 87

Nana wanted me to wash her hair. Actually, I wanted to wash her hair because it hadn't been done since she came here. Nana's hair dropped almost to her waist, so to wash this mane was no small task. Even though her hair has thinned considerably over the years, it was so long that to wash and dry it took hours. I took her to the hair dresser last year, but she did not like that. I didn't really know why. I think she felt uncomfortable with her head back in a sink that looks like a urinal. It also occurred to me that she never went to the hairdresser, ever. That's why her hair was like an ancient Lady Godiva. She always had it up in a bun or a braid. The only time I saw her with a different hairstyle was in the pictures of her in the Roaring Twenties when she was a sassy young girl with a bob working at the seashore. Wonder if she would consider the "sassy look" again? But no, she refused to go back to the salon and insisted that I was perfectly capable of handling the job.

First, we had to decide where to do this. I couldn't have her kneel next to the tub and bend forward because it would hurt her knees. She couldn't stay on her knees with her head in the upside down position long enough to scrub her scalp and wash the rest of the length of her hair. I knew this because we tried it. We got the top of her head wet and she sat back whimpering for me to stop with water dripping all over her housecoat and the floor.

Next we tried the kitchen sink, but I couldn't find a chair high enough to get her head at sink level so she could lean backwards so I could wash her hair with the vegetable squirter. She gagged every time I leaned her head back because she was too short. I ended up squirting most of the kitchen and plenty of Rachel, who thought this a marvelous game.

I took her to the laundry tub in the laundry room and made her stand with her hair bent over her head which hung over the tub. This was fine until the edge of the tub started digging into her ligaments, and we had to stop. Her ligaments, you say? Every time Nana had a pain or we made her laugh too hard, she would grab her side and say: "Oh my ligaments; stop my ligaments hurt!" So when something hurt her, we just called it her ligaments. I didn't know what the hell it meant, but it worked for her, and I knew she was in pain or laughing her ass off.

I pushed her pretty hard on the ligaments thing to get this hair clean. I was almost there. One last rinse, and I think I could have finished. But no...so now she had a head full of soapy hair and we just had to find a way to finish this thing. I considered taking her out and squirting her with the garden hose, but in thirty degree weather that might have been considered elder abuse. Of course, she might have tolerated a bit of inconvenience if she knew what was coming.

Finally, I just damn well insisted that we all get naked and get in the shower together. I had a seat in there and two shower heads, and that's where we completed the task. You may wonder why I didn't just do that in the first place. Three women naked in the shower in all stages of bodily creation was not my idea of a good time. I think I was afraid of what I might see of my future, and I didn't want to look. It was not a pretty sight. Breasts pointing to the floor, an ass seemingly having a conversation with said breasts, as they were both below sea level, and general sagging at every turn. The only good thing was that Nana is practically hairless everywhere, and I mean everywhere, so *there's* something to look forward to...savings on razor blades.

Listening to Rachel's chuckles as she showered with her homies, reminded me of all the long luxurious baths Nana lorded over when I was little. We seemed to be in that tub for hours with at least one sibling and a lot of Mr. Bubble. Part of me now realized that was probably the moment in time when she was folding laundry or making beds or some other chore, since there were always at least two or three of us in the tub. I also realized that it's very biblical to wash one another—isn't it? The whole routine of washing, cleansing, starting anew has restorative powers each and every time. I was blessed to be returning and reliving the favor from Nana and passing it on to my daughter. For just a moment, the water felt fresh and new and comforting with a bevy of family females.

Rachel enjoyed the adventure. It was like going to a swim party in the middle of winter with your mommy and great-grandmother. Whooppee.

DAY 88

Rachel and Nana were committing mutiny. I considered that they were having union meetings during naptime. They presented their demands. They wanted a shorter nap time.

"No nap, Mommy," Rachel cried.

"Yeah, honey girl, no nap," Nana joined in.

"Girls, you need a nap. You're cranky. I'm cranky. We're all much better behaved after nap time. Besides, you girls like to go to your rooms for quiet time, don't you?"

"Nana," I reminded her, "you're always saying how much you like to lie down in your room and read for a bit in the afternoon. Just because you happen to fall asleep means you need some rest. I'm not *making* you take a nap."

"Well," she said sheepishly, "I suppose that's true."

"And Rachel…" I paused, I didn't have any logical answer for a two-year-old that would make her agree. Two-year-olds don't live by logic. They live by their own moral code which says, "This is what I want to do when I want to do it, and I will fight to the death for my right to do it." Nana, was in fact, the easier of the two to convince.

"Well, Rachel you just have to go to bed. You're two," I said.

"Waaaaaah," Rachel said with a sideways glance at her union rep.

"Now see what you've done, honey girl. There, there, Rachel, she didn't mean it," Nana said.

"Maybe we can take a nap every other day," said Nana. The negotiations had begun.

"No," I said, "that's impossible. Maybe you could take a nap without complaining or getting the child all riled up," I retorted.

"No, I don't think so," she said as she winked at her rank and file. Well, it was only rank; she didn't have any file. Rachel winked back by blinking both her eyes and nodding her head severely.

"How about this?" I suggested. "What if you get to choose your nap time as long as it's between eleven and two o'clock?"

"That sounds reasonable," said Nana, "but I think we should get a reprieve if we're at the mall—or shopping."

"Reprieve, hmmm..." I said. Where did she get this stuff? It must be the damn cryptoquote or crossword puzzles. Perhaps they had secret messages in them from the national sisterhood that instructed them how to craftily handle management on critical issues.

"Well, okay, no naps on those days, but if and only IF we are not home by two AND you go to bed by seven-thirty." Aha! I had her. She'd never agree to that. Since the union member didn't tell time, she could sell her out, but she'd have to sell herself out as well. I was feeling pretty crafty myself.

"Okay, deal, but we don't get punished or have to go back to bed if we get up before six the next morning."

Trump. I was undone. I could not get up with these hooligans before 6 A.M.

Well, I had two ways to go. I could stop all negotiations now, or I could agree to the terms and hope they forgot by the next time we went to the mall. Or I could just make sure I was never—and I mean never—out at two o'clock in the afternoon. Then I realized with a sense of great relief that I did indeed have one more option. It was miraculous; it was foolproof; and there was no higher authority—at least in Nana's mind.

"Well, that sounds good to me, Nana, and I would love to agree to that here and now and end all this silliness, but I can only give you a tentative agreement because (drum roll please) *I have to get John's permission!"*

"Well, of course, honey girl, I wouldn't have it any other way," she said sweetly.

"Now, according to our tentative contract, you girls have to go to bed now, and we'll talk to Daddy when he gets home," I said in a kind but firm voice.

"Okay," they said in unison, and trudged up the stairs hand-in-hand.

They were giggling as I was running to the phone to call John and tell him not to DARE allow them the pre-six o'clock condition of nap time. He would think the whole thing was crazy, but every once in a while you had to let the troops think they had some control.

DAY 89

Reading was a treat that was pretty much denied me during this time. There really was no time for reading, not in the concentration sense of the word. I could read a label. All good mothers read labels—you know, for sugar content and calories and grams of fat. I could read "Elmo Takes A Bath" over and over and over again. I had to read the pill bottles for Nana's medication. I even had time to study the TV Guide for optimal PBS programming to entertain all parties simultaneously. On nights when I would drop into bed before ten o'clock, I might pick up a magazine or even a book, but then of course, it was time for sex. That is why I had not read anything of significance—ever. Nobody wanted me to read. They knew that if I were reading, I was not paying attention to them. If I could possibly follow the plot of a book that was more than ten pages long, I had given myself over to another realm. That was unacceptable, as everyone in this house had needs that involved me. Moreover, those who lived with me were justifiably afraid that I might find out through extensive reading that in the big world out there, people were sane and having fun.

I suppose we were having fun. They would say funny things all the time—sometimes to me; sometimes to each other.

"Come here, honey girl, you need your pants changed," Nana would say to Rachel.

"You don't like my pants?" Rachel asked Nana with all sincerity.

"Of course, I like your pants, I mean your diaper."

"Oh, you don't like my diaper. Okay you can have it now."

Those were the times Nana and I were a team. We laughed in unison.

"Does this remind you of when I was little?"

"No, not really."

Well, so much for that sentimental moment.

The phone rang. It was my mother. She was lucky that it was a good time. We were in the midst of laughing.

"What's so funny?" my mother said.

"I wish I could remember," I said.

"I'm just so surprised, most of the time you don't answer. If you do you're stressed beyond comprehension. It's nice to hear you laugh."

"Yes, you're right. How are you?"

"Fine. It's sunny. It's warm. It's got its ups and downs. How are you?"

"Oh just fine. It's cloudy. It's freezing. It's a crap shoot every day between hysteria and insanity."

"There's my girl. Seriously, how's your grandmother?"

"Actually, except for the dreaded incontinence, she's doing pretty well. I don't think she misses you anymore."

"Thank God for that."

"Yeah, but how are we going to get her home in the summer?"

"Well, maybe she'll just stay with you," my mother said just a bit too brightly.

Silence. Dead Silence.

"Cathy?"

Nothing.

"Cathy, I'm only kidding. Don't be ridiculous. Of course, she's coming home. For heaven's sake, breathe will you."

I took a deep breath.

"Sorry, you scared me."

"Who knows better than I what you're going through. It was just a joke."

"But Mom, it's a proven fact that you have no sense of humor."

"Ha, ha. Very funny. Let me talk to Nana."

"Okay, but how about you talk to Rachel first, she's chomping at the bit to get on the phone."

"Well, why didn't you say so?" "Hi honey, it's Nanny. How are you?"

For some reason my mother had decided to be called "Nanny" by her grandchildren. When she started this fifteen years ago with my nephews, she did so not thinking that her mother would live that long, and so it would be a tribute to Nana to carry on a derivation of her "name." So now each grandchild that comes along has to learn the difference between Nana and Nanny.

"Goooood."

"Are you being a good girl for Mommy?"

"Yeeeees."

"Do you have anything to tell me?"

"Nooooo."

"Okay, can I talk to Nana now?"

"Okay. Nanny?"

"Yes?"

"I can poo poo in the potty."

"Well aren't you a very good girl."

"Not every time."

"Well, yes that takes practice doesn't it?"

"Okay, bye."

Rachel dropped the phone, and it bounced on the floor two or three times.

"Sorry, Mom, here's Nana."

"Hello?"

"Hello, Mother, it's me Mary Ann."

"Are you home?"

"No, I'm still in Florida."

"Okay, well take care."

Nana hands me the phone.

"Apparently, you're doing just fine, dear."

"Don't let them fool you, Mom. It's their daily shot of Benadryl, right before nap time."

"CATHY...!"

"I'm the one with the sense of humor, remember?"

"Talk to you soon. I love you. Especially for doing this. I know how hard it is. Your mother needed this much needed break. Take care, honey. I'll call you in a few days."

"Bye Mom."

She hung up, and I cried. Hard. I think I just wanted my Mommy.

DAY 90

This is what I did today:

Got Rachel out of her crib.

Took the dog for a walk.

Gave Rachel and Nana breakfast.

Did two loads of laundry.

Cleaned up the kitchen at least three times.

Emptied the dishwasher.

Cleaned up the family room.

Built a fire for heat... twice.

Suited Rachel up in snowsuit, gloves, boots, scarf and mittens so we could go out and play in the snow.

Threw stick to dog one thousand times.

Worked on a writing project.

Helped Rachel color.

Read a book to Rachel.

Gave Rachel and Nana lunch.

Put Rachel to bed for a nap.

Skied on cross-country ski machine.

Worked on writing project.

Took shower, washed and dried hair and got dressed (no sweatshirt, real clothes).

Made pot of soup from scratch for Nana's and Rachel's supper.

Got trash together and took it down to end of that very long driveway.

Put Rachel and Troon in the car to go fetch the mail.

Got changed to go out for dinner.

It was now only 5:30 P.M.

I am woman; hear me roar!

DAY 91

I went to church this day by myself. It was a very early morning Mass, so the only ones there were the elderly, the nuns and a few people my age. There were so few people that the church remained cold and barren throughout the service.

But it occurred to me during Mass that these people were here every Sunday, and I knew a lot of them were here every day. My mother goes to Mass every day *but* Sunday. She likes the Saturday night rule where you can now go to church on Saturday night, make a debacle of yourself all over town and sleep in on Sunday morning and not feel guilty. Of course, my mom is not making a debacle of herself, at least not that I know of. She just likes a quick and pure Mass without a lot of singing or "hocus pocus," as she calls it. It's just a bit too holy for her on Sunday what with the congregation having to chime in every five minutes. Just give me my damn Mass and let me go home, is what I *think* she's thinking. Maybe that's not quite accurate. But certainly, these daily worshipers were a different breed than the only Sunday set. They were really here to pray. I guess the rest of us do the same one day a week, but these people were serious. And then I realized—they were praying for me. They may have had their own intentions, or they may have been there without any specific intention, but each and every prayer they made was somehow for their community of which I am a part. A small part, probably a lousy part on any given day, but a part to be prayed for.

These people were here every day to make the world a better place, and I am a part of that world. On the weekdays, the average age at Mass was clearly between 70 and 80. These ancient ancestors were honoring us while they were still here. They were taking a bit of their time to connect the dots of a crazy world in a spiritual way. They worked at praying because they knew this was important work. Their lives were such now that they had time and mental wherewithal to credit their Creator with His due and ask for his guidance and light.

I needed these prayers. I would see Nana praying. I didn't usually realize it. I would jump to the conclusion that something needed fixing if she were in a meditative state. If I caught her lying down at an odd moment, or she would get up in the morning much later than usual, I would ask her what the problem is.

"I was just praying, honey girl," she would say calmly.

"For what?" I always asked.

"Just praying, honey girl, that's all," she sighed.

Her sigh told me that she thought I didn't get it, and until this bit of time I took for Mass, I think she was absolutely right. I realized real praying was a privilege of the elderly. They had earned the right through time and life's trials to enjoy the comfort of prayer, the power of prayer. They had the secret knowledge that prayer was doing them good or it's doing someone else some good somewhere, perhaps in a place they would never know. But it didn't matter. It's prayer and it's good and it works because I'm 70 or 80 or 90 or 92, and I'm still here with a roof over my head and food on my table.

As Mass ended, and we were to "go in peace," I became very emotional. I was teary and uncertain as to why. Bundling up against the cold wind as I walked to my car, I realized that in her moments of grace, Nana was praying for me. She was taking a bit of time out of her precious hours left and praying for me and everyone in my household. They were all praying for me, and they were praying for you. Every prayer in that church every day was for all of us to go in peace. What a good and very unworthy feeling.

DAY 92

The real world was falling apart. There was talk of war. My friends were frightening me. As a mother, this horrified me. Yet, as an adult, I realized that there was always talk of war. How it touched you could be intimate or foreign. But there was always war. Then there was Nana's point of view. She had lived through two World Wars, the Korean War, and the Vietnam War. In the first war, she was in her teens. In the Second World War, my mother was in her teens and Nana was in her forties. During the Korean War, my mother met my father at an Army hospital. He was an injured soldier, and she was a nurse. During the Vietnam war, my brother missed the draft by one year.

I wanted to know her thoughts.

"Nana?"

"Yes, honey girl."

"Have you been reading the paper?"

"Of course, you know I do the cryptoquote and the puzzle every day."

"No, I mean the rest of the paper."

"Well, of course. How do you think I learn anything?"

Never be fooled by the elderly. They are as diverse as the rest of the population. Just because she didn't share her every thought with me didn't mean she wasn't thinking.

"I'm sorry. I just wanted to know what you thought about all this talk of war in the Gulf."

"Well, let me tell you something, honey girl. I have been through two World Wars, the Korean War, and the Vietnam War. I have seen this country respond to war in ways that would make you proud and ways that would shame you, but what I know for a fact is that war has its advantages and its drawbacks.

"We women would never have been allowed to work like we did if it weren't for the Second World War. Although most people forget, or they're dead, that we women worked in the First World War too. So it was a lot easier to feed my family even after the war, since men would still hire a good worker.

"Of course, the downside is the dead boys. We don't forget, honey girl. A lot of sadness goes along with the word patriotism. But life goes on. And what can you do? Lots of people live with tragedy every day. This is life. It happens. You have to taste it, and you have to take it. But if I had my druthers, I'd go for the patriotic side of war. It was a lot better than those crazy hippies of the Vietnam time. And those boys suffered twice—there and here. I don't think that was right, honey girl. You give to your country, your country should respect that and get behind you. Your daddy gave the ultimate sacrifice, and it wasn't even a war. I don't like war, darling, but I do like to feel proud of my country and the people who serve it. It isn't often we get that opportunity anymore. Does that answer your question?"

I nodded yes. I was speechless. I really missed *that* Nana.

Her completely lucid explanation of a view on war reminded me so much of her guidance and love as a teenager. I always thought Nana was smart. I often told her, her failure to become a teacher as she'd dreamed, didn't fail at all. She just had a smaller classroom of six. She was teaching us all the time.

Nana was, at least to my mind, always in the moment with her grandchildren. She wasn't telling us to look to the future or muddle in the past, she was just there to guide and protect. If the situation called for you to also be in the moment, and look at your own behavior as falling short, she was there to give you your comeuppance. Yet, her discipline was so brilliant. It was just a mirror shined onto your behavior. She saved this tool for the teen and pre-teen years. I don't think any one of us escaped, but each of us has their own story of shame.

This memory came to me. When I was 11-years-old, I started to become a little sassy. The kids of today are ever so much worse than what I mean. The worst things I probably did were to roll my eyes at my mother or Nana, or maybe I would "forget" to do a chore and then complain about it. I can assure you I never once said a blatant "No" to either Mom or my Nana. But for me and for that time, it was quite bold. In fact, that was the expression Nana used and continued to use to describe this behavior.

"Don't be so bold, honey girl."

It meant smart-mouthed, or sarcastic in a cutting and rude manner. And I clearly remember at 11-years-old my grandmother saying to me:

"You used to be such a nice girl."

This cut me to the quick. I couldn't imagine Nana thinking that I wasn't a nice girl. I was a nice girl. I was just testing the waters. I was a middle child. No one looked at me unless I made them. I was always the peacemaker. Why did I have to be the nice one all the time? Maybe that's why I wanted to be a lawyer, so I could yell at people and be respected. Or so people would pay attention to me, the bold and outspoken lawyer. It didn't work out that way either. I was known in my office to the lawyers, staff and clients as "the nice one."

But that one remark from Nana, probably made me the nice one forever.

DAY 93

Nana had been sick for days. I had to call the doctor. Just try and get a doctor to do a house call these days. But I really insisted. Besides, getting her and Rachel in the car to go sit in a doctor's office would be out of the question. Especially since her symptoms were that she was losing her bowels all over the house. Yes, I am not kidding. I was even cleaning shit from the walls of my bathroom. I was washing sheets and towels three and four times a day. It was horrifying. I was trapped.

This appeared to be a constant theme during Nana's stay. But that was her nemesis. Some old people just forget everything they do. Others pee themselves constantly. Some drool, or can't speak, or forget their teeth or won't change their clothes. Nana shits. It was vulgar, but there's no candy coating this life of a caregiver. It's the same for young mothers. We just got to call it poo-poo. Changing diapers was expected. We lived with the smell and the mess because that's what babies do.

Well guess what? That's what old people do too. If you're lucky enough to become one of them, it just might be you. Your dignity will be compromised, and your life will smell.

So the doctor finally arrived.

"What seems to be the problem?" he asked.

I thought, "What? You can't smell the problem?"

However, I maintained my composure, in light of the miracle that there was a doctor in my house.

"I believe it may be her diverticulitis."

"Well, let's go see the patient."

"Hello, Margaret, I'm Dr. Keene. How are you?"

"I beshit myself."

By the way, I really hate when doctors call themselves "Dr. So-and-So" and believe they can refer to a 92-year-old lady by her first name. What happened to respect? I know this is an ongoing theme with me, but I just don't understand why and when we lose respect. I would never call a doctor I just met by his first name. Are they learning this in medical school: "Just call everyone by their first name??" It's easier for you and seems cozy for the patient!" I know this pet peeve makes little sense, but it's just that you lose so much dignity with old age. Would it kill you to just ASK if you can call her by her first name? This guy wasn't even born when my grandmother, *MRS. REPKO*, was working her tail off during the Depression to keep food in the mouths of her four children. So what the hell, Nana, talk "shit" with this doctor all you want.

He examined her, and we went down to the kitchen to discuss her condition.

"Yes, I do believe it's a flare up of her diverticulitis."

"Good. So can you give me a prescription?"

He started to write out the prescriptions on his pad in totally unintelligible handwriting.

"This will help with the spasms. And I'll give you something to help with the diarrhea."

"What about the pain? She really could use some codeine or Percocet, something like that."

"Oh, we don't like to prescribe that too readily. It is addictive you know."

Okay, this was where I lost *my* shit.

"I have been listening to moaning and agony for three days. This poor old lady can barely get out of her bed to get to the bathroom on time. In fact, she can't. I have been cleaning brown off every available surface from her room to the bathroom. All the while she is in abject pain. Do you really think she or I care if she becomes a codeine addict over the next ten days? Do you really believe that I am going to let you leave this house without a prescription for a pain killer while a 92-year-old woman is interminably suffering?"

I think he recognized the look in my eye as one similar to a cheetah on the hunt for prey.

"Of course, Cathy, I just wanted you to understand the dangers of narcotics for Margaret."

He handed me the prescription, knowing full well he was in much more dangerous territory than any drug dealer with a junkie who needed a fix.

"Thank you. And by the way Jim, my grandmother's name is Mrs. Repko, and my name is Mrs. Sikorski. Have a nice day."

Isn't being old enough? Why do we have to torture them too?

DAY 95

Nana was feeling so much better; she was following me around the house like a puppy. I had to think up chores for her to keep her entertained. Rachel and Troon also followed the circuitous route around the house. The house wasn't that big. We looked like a Family Circus cartoon.

Nana decided she needed to help more around the house. She really felt very badly about the fact that she didn't have better control of herself while she was ill. She knew it was difficult. Sometimes she remembered how hard it was to be a domestic goddess. So in her efforts to assist me, she decided to build a fire in the wood burning stove. It was frigid in the family room, even on warm winter days. When the house was built, the family room was an after-thought, and the wood burning stove was added because the heating system of two small vents in one corner of the room was clearly insufficient. This kept no one warm with the exception of the occasional mouse.

As I was upstairs giving Rachel a nice warm bath, Nana was downstairs devising a plan for a cozy afternoon folding laundry by the fireside. I heard suspicious noises. I called downstairs.

"Nana?"

Nothing. I went to the top of the stairs where I could still keep an eye on Rachel as she alternately washed Barbie's hair and her own hair.

"Nana?"

Like she could hear me.

"NANA!"

"I can't hear you, honey girl."

"Come to the stairs."

"What?"

"Please come to the stairs."

"I can't hear you, honey girl."

Since I had read every disaster story in every women's and parents' magazine, I knew if I went down even one step, Rachel would drown. If I did not go downstairs, whatever those strange noises were would come to haunt me sooner or later.

I grabbed a towel.

"No, Mommy, I not ready."

"I'll put you right back, honey. Mommy just wants to help Nana for a second."

"No, Mommy. Tell Nana wait a secon'."

"I promise, honey, we'll come right back. Barbie will wait. Tell her to wait just one minute."

Rachel started crying.

"Oh for heaven's sake."

I grabbed her out of the tub. She fought like a banshee kicking and screaming all the way down the stairs. I ran into the family room. There was Nana about to light the fire. She had placed one piece of wood, the size of Rhode Island, one piece of writing paper, and a Bounce sheet into the stove. The match was poised in her hand.

"NO!"

Of course, if she had any left, this would have scared the shit out of her. As it was, she just jumped pretty well for an old broad.

"Sorry, Nana. But could you come upstairs and help with Rachel's bath? Then I can start the fire so it's toasty warm when she's done."

"No, don't want Nana."

"Of course I can, honey girl, why didn't you say so?"

Nana was unmoved when a grandchild would say he or she didn't want to have anything to do with her.

We retreated to the bathroom where I supervised for a short while. Everyone seemed to be getting along just ducky. So I quickly went downstairs, removed Nana's fire apparatus from the stove and built a nice blazing fire. It was going quite well when I rushed back to the bathroom and found the two cohorts in crime splashing all over the place. Nana had become a fan of the whipped cream soap in a can. It was in their hair, on Nana's glasses, dripping down the shower curtain and all over the tub. To be honest with you, I was a bit jealous. I used to love that foamy in a can bath soap for kids. When we discovered that on TV, we were relentless in begging Mom and Nana for a can...just one can...of whipped cream soap. I don't know how six of us collectively thought that *one can* of whipped soap would satisfy all our squirting needs, but we got that can. Then the bathers realized: "Hey wait, we actually WANT to take a bath because of this crazy soap." So getting us in the tub was much easier. Now, getting us out of the tub? That was a different story. And so it went. But the other upside was we squirted that soap everywhere in that bathroom, and had to wipe it all off before we could leave the bathroom. So, the kids actually ended up cleaning the bathroom with every trip to the tub.

Since it was only Rachel and Nana, I was not getting the full-on crazy soap everywhere, but there was definitely an upside.

"Nana fun, Mommy."

"Don't I know it, little one!"

The day was good. We ate, we folded laundry. I put Rachel down for her nap. I came back to the family room where Nana had placed five large logs in the fireplace thus killing the fire and causing the smoke alarm to spew its scream all over the neighborhood. And this really was a good day.

DAY 97

The things that Nana taught me when I was a child:

Make your bed.

Do the right thing.

Fight your own battles.

Wear clean underwear—you never know what might happen.

Clean up the kitchen.

Spring cleaning AND Fall cleaning.

Be nice to the kids at school that nobody likes.

Don't steal.

Go to church.

Say your prayers.

Kissing a boo boo works.

Fight nice.

Wear a little lipstick.

Mind your manners.

Life is hard.

Life is good.

Do your homework.

Cooking is love.

Crying is okay.

Never underestimate the power of a good hug.

Hold in your stomach.

Respect your elders.

Make jokes.

Take a joke.

Laugh loud and often.

Be kind.

Be careful.

Be good.

A stiff prick knows no conscience.

About that last one…these were Nana's parting words to me when I left for college. She wanted me to understand that I should be careful and not fall for a boy without understanding where he might be coming from. This is so interesting to me now, since I know that Nana "had" to get married. After dating my Pop Pop for *ten* years, she finally, at age 28 in 1927, made the decision that there was only one way to get this sonavabitch to marry her. Of course, it is impressive that she did NOT get pregnant for ten years! So it was an age appropriate statement to make to me on my way to college. Sort of, but not really for a Catholic school girl, who took to heart all the other lessons I just reiterated, and who was truly afraid that she was being called every night to be a nun, since all the nuns told us that being a nun was a "calling." But all were good lessons, every one of them, especially the one about holding in your stomach.

DAY 100

Isn't day 100, the day the President calls a big press conference or State of the Union address just to let everyone know how he's doing so far. Wouldn't it be great if he called the conference and said:

"You know, my fellow Americans, this job sucks. I'll keep tryin' it 'cause after all I am the President, but man, no one told me how crappy this job was really gonna be. I'm supposed to have all the answers. And when I mess up everyone blames me for everything. For God's sake, I wasn't even the President until three months ago. How am I supposed to have created this mess that quickly? And then you want me to clean it up? I'm doing my best. Hang in there. And there you have it. Thank you."

Our one hundred days was much like that.

To celebrate the fact that no one has died or required serious hospitalization (except for that blood transfusion thing, which we were trying to forget), I decided to take the girls shopping for bathing suits. Well, not Nana. She doesn't swim. She never did swim as far as I could remember. Yet, we spent our entire summers at the swimming pool from dawn till way past dusk. But it never occurred to me until now that Nana never left the shallow end. Neither did my mother, but that was because she didn't want to muss—yes, that is the proper word—"muss" her hairdo. That was what all the mothers did. But Nana only came to the pool to watch us in the swim meets and rarely to spend an afternoon.

Summer at the pool was our day camp. In those days, all kinds of mothers stayed at the pool with their kids and watched whoever was there. They were like camp counselors who did not entertain, only discipline. We started at 8 A.M. with swim team practice and hot chocolate in the freezing mornings of the early summer. We left the pool around 9 or 10 P.M. with pruny skin and eyes so chlorinated, we thought the rainbow colored rings around the pool lights and headlights going home were a natural phenomenon, like the aurora borealis, only in Pennsylvania.

Nana hardly ever came to the pool. She was glad she had never learned to swim because this was an excuse for her rest period. During the summer, all six of us were home at the same time. Maybe she was an Olympic quality swimmer but kept that little secret to herself. It all makes complete sense to me now. She and my mother insisted that we take lessons and be on the swim team by the time each one of us reached the age of six. All of us are proficient swimmers now. My eldest brother is a winning swim team coach, and my youngest brother became quite an accomplished surfer. In my heyday, I would swim at least a mile a day just for exercise. I used to find it hard to believe that my mother and Nana couldn't swim. But I was on to them—now that they were in their sixties and nineties. Oh, they're good; they were really good.

So, we entered the bathing suit adventure. Even at two years old, Rachel had very specific opinions about fashion. Nana also retained certain opinions. Quelle surprise!

"I don't like that one, Mommy," Rachel told me in no uncertain terms.

"Just try it on, honey, so we can see the size."

"No, I don't like it."

"Fine."

"How about this one?"

"No."

I held the suits up one by one for approval or disapproval.

"This one?"

"hmm-mm."

"Oh, this one's adorable."

"Don't like ordable."

Now the expert took charge of the reins.

"Honey girl?"

"What?" Rachel and I said together.

"I was talking to Rachel."

Rachel looked up at Nana with her big brown eyes, a look of triumph on her face. "If you don't try on a bathing suit right now, we're going home."

Hopes dashed.

"Okay."

I was continually cowed by the expert when she appeared like *The Three Faces of Eve.*

Rachel tried on every single suit in the store and chose the first one I held up. We were all exhausted. Even though Nana and I were just observers of the two-year-old runway model with every swimsuit, we too wished to go home. Another lesson as to why you should limit the choices of all two year olds. Don't be fooled. There was a method to my madness. Tired toddlers and nappy Nanas made for great afternoon companions.

DAY 101

Seventy-nine days to go.

DAY 102

I got sick. I couldn't breathe. I couldn't sleep—not that they would have let me anyway. And I was miserable. Yes, they had now become "they." It was me against them. Do you think it mattered to them that I was sick? Heavens no. I was still expected to perform at the highest level of accomplishment. I was still expected to make all meals…real meals and not cereal or toast for breakfast, but hot cereal and brewed coffee.

I hated them. Okay, I said it. But give me a break; I was sick. I was coughing constantly. Used tissues were scattered all over the house like some crazed manna from heaven. But it's the opposite of manna, because I had to clean it up, not eat it. I had to prevent the dog, Troon, from eating it, and the child from playing with it. It's anti-manna.

Nana tried to help, but I hated her too. Her help made everything worse. If I would lie down, she wanted to feed someone or something. She tried to fill the washer, dryer, dishwasher, trash can, wood-burning stove, diaper pail, dog dish or any other vessel she came across with anything that seemed appropriate. This never worked. I ended up following her around to keep clean clothes out of the washer, clean diapers out of the trash can, dirty dishes out of a dishwasher full of clean dishes—which meant I must empty the dishwasher immediately as per Nana's instructions. I was exhausted.

Where was my husband? Working, of course. He was no dummy. Work had become the refuge he always dreamed it would be. He loved to go to work now. It was exhilarating. He was hardly tired when he returned home. Or perhaps I was so tired that no one looked tired to me anymore.

I had no help. My sisters were busy. They worked full time and had their own families. I didn't think this would be so hard. How could this be so hard? Nana was an adult. We only had one child in the house. But they were making me want to crawl in a hole and pull the dirt over the top. It was the demands. The constant demands. Feed me. Change me. Entertain me. Keep me safe. Bathe me. Shop for me. Play with me. What about me, me?

DAY 104

Oh my God, who would ever believe all that disgusting whining I wrote two days ago! It was the Nyquil talking. I had no business complaining like that. Nobody had cancer. Well, Cindy had cancer, but we were dealing with that too, and that's not what I was complaining about. Okay, it was hard, and it was all true in the moment. But I felt very much better than I did. Now I was having Oprah guilt. She was out there telling us we all needed to be grateful and that we should be writing in our grateful journals everyday and how we have so much to be thankful for. So I tried to behave myself.

I am grateful for my healthy child.

I am grateful for my wonderful understanding husband.

I am grateful for the time Nana gave to me as a child.

I am grateful for this nice house.

I am grateful for the rainy day.

I am grateful forrrr…

I couldn't finish that because of the loud crash. I ran downstairs to find Nana up from her nap, standing on a kitchen chair trying to get the flour off the top shelf so she could bake some pies. I am grateful that she didn't fall off the stool. I am grateful that she only dropped the flour onto the dish drainer. I am grateful that she only broke a few glasses. I am grateful that I didn't kill her.

DAY 110

The sun was shining with a vengeance. It was momentarily springtime. We all had the fever of spring. It was delicious. We were outside. We were free from the enclosures of winter. Enough with the "cozy" as we were all saying "Let us out in the mud, the sticks, the gravel, and the mulch. We were going *aplanting* this week." It would be a gargantuan endeavor. Usually, I plant three or four hundred flowers in the spring. Shade envelops my entire yard, with one exception, where I plant a few tomatoes and peppers. This season, my evil assistants would be helping with the beautification project.

Most of the real planting would be done during naptime. But in order to get these two some fresh air and make them tired, I enlisted them as garden gnomes—I mean assistants. Nana had done this job many times. So, she knew her way around a trowel. It's what she forgot that was frustrating, dangerous and downright scary.

We began with our wardrobes. I have never seen Nana wear pants a day in her life. My mom told me that during World War II, Nana wore pants to work because that's what everyone was doing, but since then, she was strictly a dress person. There was nothing dramatic about these dresses. They were certainly not cocktail attire. But for some reason, she preferred a dress. A dress also meant stockings and shoes with heels. Nana did not believe in pantyhose. She wore garters, not the sexy Victoria's Secret kind but the elastic bands that are about three inches thick and sit right above the knee kind. And even though the heels on her shoes were "serviceable" which meant they were two inches thick all the way around, they would still sink her into the mud like a shipwreck.

I tried to entice her to at least wear my garden clogs. But after a sashay around the kitchen that looked like she'd been nipping at the vodka, we agreed to let her wear her own shoes. This prompted Rachel to want to garden in her Cinderella slippers. Round one—the interlopers.

Off we went in tiaras and heels to the garden. Earlier in the morning, I had arranged the trowels, watering cans, plants, hose and fertilizer for easy access. Rachel ran right to the flower flats and started pulling out impatiens by their pretty little budded heads. Now they were decapitated. What did I do in response to this?

"NO! DO NOT DO THAT RACHEL!" not in my kindest voice.

What did Rachel, a little, excited two year old who is trying to help her Mommy do? Cried like a banshee.

Who was the worst mother on the planet?

Nana reminded me, "She was only trying to help, honey girl."

Sheepishly I said, "I know, Nana, I'm so sorry."

"Don't apologize to me, you didn't yell at me this time."

Ouch.

I scooped up the injured soldier and hugged and kissed her tears away, apologized profusely, and we started all over again.

"Now, Mommy will dig the holes with Rachel. And then Nana can take the flowers out of the planters and hand them to us so we can put them in the ground."

"No, Mommy. I do the flowers," said Princess Rachel adjusting her tiara as it flopped over her eyes.

"Rachel, let's try it this way first and see how it works."

"But, Mommy…."

I put the trowel in her hand and helped her dig a hole. Instantaneously, a big fat worm crawled on to the trowel and toward her pudgy little hand.

"AAAHHHH," she said.

"It's only a worm," I said. Meanwhile inside I'm saying "AAAHHH".

"No worms, Mommy. Don't like it."

Quite frankly, neither did I. I relented.

"Okay, you help Nana with the flowers, while I dig the hole."

We had been outside for thirty minutes and had yet to plant one flower. We commenced. I dug about ten holes as quickly as possible. They got into the swing of things pretty quickly, and began to hand me the flowers one by one. Henry Ford was right about assembly lines. This one worked for a while until Nana decided it was time to fill the watering cans. While my back was turned, she picked up the hose and put it in the watering can. She squeezed the nozzle. The watering can went flying across the driveway. Water shot across Rachel's tiara which took flight into the dogwood tree, and sent a lovely sluice up my back.

"That's it! Planting is over!" I declared with the authority of a despot.

Nana and Rachel erupted in the giggles. Nana harbored that gleam in her blue-grey eyes, and I couldn't believe what I thought was going to happen next. She aimed that hose right at us and squirted again. Rachel screamed with pure relish. I was yelling.

"Stop that! You stop that right now!"

No use. They were having too much fun.

This continued for awhile. All their clothes got sufficiently soaked. Now it was getting a bit cold out there, and the plants were starting to be attacked as well.

"Okay, that's it. Fun's over!" Wow, did I say that? I hated when my Mom used to say that. Why was the fun over? The fun should never be over.

When did I stop seeing the fun?

They laughed all through cleaning up and getting into their beds for a nap. My house was filled with peals of joy. Even the dog barked a happy bark.

I went outside in the quiet and planted three hundred flowers as fast as I could with a tiara on my head and a soaking wet t-shirt.

DAY 111

Did you know that in bowling this number is called the shithouse? An old boyfriend told me that. I couldn't even remember what an old boyfriend is like, but I had no problem envisioning a shithouse. What did it feel like to be pert and perky, with boys calling and coming to your house? I sounded like something out of a Tennessee Williams play. It's not that I missed just being an adult. One misses being a person, a person of their own choosing. I felt like choice had all but disappeared. Nana would say, "You've made your bed now lie in it." I would have loved to lie in it. I couldn't. I had to get up. Oh, and I hadn't made it either; I hardly ever did.

Back to the day known as 111 or that other thing. Today they decided to help me take out the trash. Going from room to room, Rachel and Nana collected the trash into one big basket. As I went to the garage with the downstairs trash, they carefully put the basket with the upstairs trash in the kitchen.

While waiting for me to praise them and take their bundle out to the large cans, they decided on a better course of action. Apparently, I took too long in the garage. They threw the trash over the back deck railing like they were on a cruise ship. Now there was trash everywhere outside. They were giggling the whole time. Then we all had to clean it up. Just another Day 111 in paradise.

The Lido deck was closed for renovations after that.

DAY 112

My brother, who lives in California, insists that we grew up in (and I still live in) a schizophrenic cancer belt. His unauthorized research is based on a review of our childhood neighborhood.

The block was filled with people who were diseased either mentally or physically. There was dementia in every other house. Mrs. Dengler, who lived in the twin attached to ours, would visit us at all hours of the night and day and claim we were in her house. When Mr. Dengler died and there was no one to retrieve her, she had to move. I have no idea where she went, but my guess is a nursing home because she had no children that I recall. I would have to ask my mom that question. I would have asked Nana but I didn't trust her memory which wasn't really fair because her long term memory was rather excellent. It was her short term memory that got us all in trouble.

There was a suicide on Hanover Street when we were kids, which of course, was never discussed. There was Mr. Parnell who would keep all of our balls if they went in his yard. He was mean. There was Mrs. O'Donnell who just yelled at us all the time. There was a family whose kids were named Porky, Tiger, Woody, Cookie and Barry. We couldn't figure out why Barry didn't get a nickname. Maybe it was a punishment. Maybe he just got lucky. And there were a couple of schizophrenics.

And as weird families moved out, other ones moved in. That would have to include us, right? But I just didn't think we qualified. It doesn't really matter. My brother, the bohemian one, the one who lives as a straight guy in San Francisco, the one who lives the least traditional lifestyle, likes to remind us that the rest of us stayed with the crazies.

I wouldn't mind so much. But now that I was spending all this time with Nana, it made me worry. What was I doing to my daughter? Was this just the aging process, or were we really exposed here in the radon belt to other unknown forces that make us all lunatics eventually? Even though we didn't live in my childhood home, we did live only a few miles away.

I consoled myself with the fact that Nana had gotten to ninety-two years of age without needing any assistance. That was good enough for me. If I get to ninety-anything and my granddaughter will put up with me, God bless us both and thanks. I just hope she doesn't yell too much.

DAY 113

Everyone seemed to have their sphincter under control so I thought we could venture another trip to the mall. It's brave, I know but time for some Easter finery!

Nana refused to buy any new clothes.

"Honey girl, I am ninety-two years old, what do I need with a new dress?"

"But it will be fun, Nana, and you'll look so nice in some bright colors," I pleaded with her.

"You just get something for you and the baby. That's what bright colors are for."

I cajoled a little more, but she was having none of it.

We started in the children's department with all the pastels of the season beckoning our dollars. I picked up a pretty little pink number and a lilac one too.

"Don't like it, Mommy. Want this one."

This shopping experience began to be reminiscent of the bathing suit fiasco. My karma teacher was doing a very poor job. I would live seven thousand lives at this point as it is obvious that I failed to learn one lesson in life from one month to the next. I must still be a cricket karmically.

The one Rachel chose had a darling little hat dangling from its sleeve and a cute little purse to boot. But it was a left over Christmas dress in red velvet on the sale rack. You know sometimes, we should just give in. But not this time.

"Honey, that's not an Easter dress, that's for Christmas when Santa comes. He already came. We need to get something pretty for the Easter Bunny."

"Honey girl," piped up Nana in the infinite wisdom that reappears from time to time. Obviously, *her* karma coach had been successful.

"Just take her in the dressing room and try the dresses on. You're the mommy, remember?"

"No, Nana," a little voice adamantly declared from the stroller, "creep criet."

Uh oh. A clear undercutting of mutual disrespect. What was a mother to do?

"All right both of you, this is what we're going to do. We're going into that dressing room and try some things on. Then we are going to Friendly's for lunch and ice cream and I don't want one more word of nastiness out of either of you."

Of course, the minute Rachel put on one pretty thing, she was twirling and whirling her way around the dressing room. I discovered that it didn't matter what color it was, as long as it had a hat and a purse we were good.

After ice cream, I just didn't have the energy to continue the search for my own Easter dress. I hadn't bought a new dress since before Rachel was born. The weight struggle depressed me, and now I didn't have the time to look at and try things on without my homeys catapulting clothes or strollers or themselves all over the store. I spied a few things and would enlist the aid of my husband to withstand a few hours of caregiving so I could shop alone. I would just like to pee alone again. It seemed so remotely delightful I dared not think about it.

Like a miracle from heaven, my husband came home early and encouraged me to go back to the mall, since I'd seen some things I liked. He even agreed to this before "the kids" went to bed. He was a knight that day.

I found the perfect frock. It was red with white polka dots. It was just adorable. Red is my signature color, and without a doubt, this dress was made just for me. The top had little puff short sleeves. It was fitted in the bodice and had a wide collar. It was made of crisp cotton that would withstand the breezes of spring. A white panel to button under the collar was optional, if you didn't want to show too much cleavage. Like hell. The skirt hugged your hips, but in a nice flirty way, not a gee-I've-had-too-much-butter way. I guessed I'd lost weight just running after these two. It was a size 8!! Is that possible? I didn't even want to know if it was missized. I considered wearing the tag on the outside.

I hadn't felt this good in a very long time. I felt cute. I felt powerful. I felt as shiny as a new penny, as Nana would say. I took this harbinger of spring and rebirth and plain darn cuteness home with me and tucked it safely in the guest room closet until the perfect opportunity would arise for its debut.

DAY 114

Spring fever was inhabiting the land. We were happy here. Not too much fighting going on these days. Perhaps we all suffered from that lack of sunshine syndrome. Daylight savings time had begun and the troops are taking to it like ducks to water.

Water had become the operative word. We watered the plants inside. We watered the plants outside. We had a glass of water after all of our watering. We washed the car—not very well—but if it involved water, it involved everyone. We gave or had baths morning, noon and night depending on how much dirt we've been involved with. Water kept us moving, entertained, clean and quenched. It seemed we had been in a drought and were loathe to return. Water flowed and with it flowed our good graces to one another. Who knew? All we needed was a little sunshine and a bit of a sprinkle, a soak, a drench.

DAY 120

Nana kept telling people that my mother kicked her out of her house. I found this frustrating and remarkably disloyal. In my efforts to repair this travesty of justice, I decided to take Nana to my mother's house and show her that no one was living there right now. No matter how many times I had explained to her that Mom was in Florida for a few months, Nana had convinced herself that it was a vast conspiracy to deprive her of her regular surroundings.

Nana had been complaining for the last few days about the cold at my house. She had insisted that I light the fireplace during the day to take the chill out of the family room. I did this to keep peace. In the meantime, Rachel and I were stripped down to our underwear, and I would pray that the UPS man wouldn't show up.

The moment we entered my mother's house I was secretly thrilled because it was freezing in there. The thermostat was set at fifty-nine degrees. I thought "Aha!" Nana will never settle for this; she'll just turn on her heel and say "Let's go home."

"My it's warm in here," Nana said.

"Mommy, I cold," said the sane one.

"Nana, it's fifty-seven degrees in here. You complain every day that my house is cold at seventy-four. What in God's name are you talking about?"

She ignored me.

Nana tip-toed around the house like we were visiting a mausoleum. She opened cabinets, the empty refrigerator and the door to her bedroom. There she saw her furniture, her summer clothes in the closet, her jewelry box and her own television. This space belonged to Nana. She wasn't a guest or a visitor here.

"See," I said through clenched teeth, "it's all empty. No one is here."

I was trying to retain my composure. Plus, I could see what she was seeing. Her home was abandoned, and she felt abandoned.

Rachel and I and Nana were freezing, but she kept strolling around the house.

"Let me see what's in the bathroom." She went into the bathroom, viewed the blue tile, the yellow sink, and the lavender towels.

"Hmmm. Looks like she's getting ready for Easter."

"Nana, Mom is *not* getting ready for Easter. Her bathroom is always these colors. She just left the lavender towels for when she comes home."

"Well, obviously, she's coming home for Easter, why else would she put out those towels?"

Lying to your Nana is ever so much harder than lying to your toddler.

"Okay," I said, "well if she's coming home for Easter, then we will see her then, and you can come home." I was so hoping that in all the up-coming Easter morning broo hah hah, she would forget we were here. But I was likely setting myself up for future harassment.

"She kicked me out and then she left," Nana said matter-of-factly.

I thought about asking her if she wanted to stay in this cold, dark empty place, but thought better of that. No good lawyer asks a question she doesn't know the answer to. A resounding "yes" would not have surprised me.

"Ugh. Nana, let's just go get some lunch, okay?"

"McDonalds. Yeahhhh!!!!" a wise voice three feet off the ground piped up.

"Well…..," she said hesitantly.

"Please, Nana…..really, let's just go. It's freezing in here."

"Yeah, Nana, peas? My hundry."

"Okay, but I want to check again at Easter," she said, asserting her independence just in case my mom came home and didn't report in.

After we came home from lunch, Nana went straight to bed and slept through the night. I couldn't decide if she was angry or depressed. Perhaps that was my fault for taking her to my mother's house. Or maybe she was just cold.

DAY 121

Mother's Day was coming, and Grandma would be joining us for a few days. This was a bonus for me. My mother-in-law, Marie, was none of the jokes you find at a comedy club. She was kind, generous and had an amazing sense of humor. At least I thought so because she found me endlessly funny and entertaining. She also loved Nana. My husband and I had been married for almost five years and dated for four years before that, so Marie had ample time to get to know Nana, and love her as well. So the "new" Nana, the one who was a bit ornery and forgetful was just a small phase to be endured.

Marie saw and knew that Margaret was still there in all her bright, amusing and wise glory. I suspected she also wanted to mine this quarry of old age to see if it's a place she would endure with grace or despise. Perhaps she even wanted to know how her son and daughter-in-law would treat her in her old age, if need be. Whatever it was, I was always grateful to have a helper who loved my "people" as much as I did.

The old ladies had a ball together, and Rachel was right in there with them. They danced to music, weeded the garden, fed the dog, walked the dog— VERY SLOWLY—which drove him doggy crazy, but he would not go far without them. Who was walking whom? I wondered.

They even attempted to play Frisbee with the dog. When Troonie was a puppy, he lived on the fenced-in deck during the day while John and I were at work. I would come home at lunch time, if I could, and throw the Frisbee off the deck, down the hill to give the dog exercise. I did it ten times, gave him a pat and went back to the office.

I must have trained my mother-in-law in this fine art. Marie was the first to pick up the Frisbee and try to wing it across the yard. It barely made it to the grassy knoll. Nana decided to take a turn. She threw it sideways into the air, and it came back like a boomerang. Not one of these three stooges could throw a Frisbee, much less do it off the deck. It landed in the flower garden. The dog was so excited to be playing with anyone, he would get that tail wagging ferociously and dig up my hostas to get to the Frisbee. Next it landed in the rose bush. The dog yelped at the thorns as he tried to pull it out. But the dog succeeded and brought the Frisbee back up on the porch and dropped it at Rachel's feet. It plopped back behind Rachel as she tried to throw it over the railing, which was taller than she. The dog just looked at her like she was Lucy, and he was Charlie Brown. All the while the three of them were laughing and giggling like school girls. The dog gave up and came in the house. They didn't even notice.

Lunch time, nap time, laundry time. It all went smoothly until dinner time. As soon as my husband walked in the door, all hell broke loose. Infants know when it is family dinner time and decide that is the best time to cry, scream, whine, and cause general havoc. It makes a first time mother feel extremely incompetent. All day long, I'd be with this charming baby who coos and cuddles. I couldn't wait for Daddy to come home to see just how darn cute this kid was. He arrived to the child from Hell. My sister's theory was that they didn't want to share you with Daddy, and so they acted out. My theory was they were all a pain in the ass.

John came home, and I was making a beautiful lasagna to go with the meatballs in the crockpot and the salad that my mother-in-law was creating.

"Hello everyone," said my amiable spouse.

Rachel ran to Daddy as did Troon. They were both at knee height, so there was a battle for who got the pets first. Daddy had two hands, but that was insufficient. Rachel pushed Troon away. Troon's tail smacked her in the cheek as he took the forbidden jump to get to Dad's face.

"Down, boy," said Daddy.

"No, Troon," said Rachel, "my Daddy."

"It's fine, Rachey," he said as he picked her up and gave Troon the evil eye of discipline.

"I want chicken," said my churlish grandmother.

Where the hell did that come from?

"I don't have any chicken, Nana," I said in my most comforting tone.

"I want chicken too," said my parrot daughter.

"Mommy will get chicken tomorrow," I said, giving my husband the eye with what I think is the universal call for help.

"Well, looks like we've had another nice day," observed my husband.

"I want chicken tonight," demanded Nana.

"Chicken, chicken, chicken," said Rachel.

"Yea," I said, "another nice day, and everyone is so looking forward to my lasagna."

"No zaaannnaa, Daddy, chicken."

"Rachey, Mommy worked really hard to make us a nice dinner, and Grandma is making a good salad. Daddy *loves* lasagna, don't you?"

"Yeesss."

I swear Nana was about to pick up her knife and fork, like a bad prison movie, and start banging with her chicken demands.

My husband, the man of the house, the *man* of the house looked her straight in the eye and said:

"We all love lasagna, don't we, Nana?"

My mother-in-law was laughing so hard the cucumber flew off the cutting board and into the dog's water.

DAY 123

Mother's Day. This day is shark infested waters. What I really, really, really wanted for Mother's Day was to be left alone. Greta Garbo had nothin' on me. I could not think of one way to get this message across. I am certain if I expressed this wish, there would be great retribution. Rachel loved Mother's Day. Daddy helped her make a card. She picked flowers from the garden. She got to get dressed up and go to dinner. She thought it was a great holiday.

Nana had sweet phone calls from my mother and my three uncles. We all went to the club for brunch. The club made a big deal of every mom as she arrived. Nana was given extra special attention, and she worked the room like a real pro. She tucked her fingers in her bun with a coquettish look, gave a girlish chuckle to the manager when he asked if she was my mother, and had a high ball from the bar to boot.

We came home, changed our clothes, took the dog for a walk, puttered around the house, and all of us managed to squeeze in a little nap. It was dandy. Now it was dinner time, and I felt like everyone was looking at me wondering what were we all supposed to do next?

Getting everyone bathed and dressed to go out; making sure the dog was walked before and after; answering the phone every fifteen minutes for calls to Nana or Marie from their children; and the biggest mistake of all, having two glasses of wine with dinner, put me over the edge. I was woozy from soup to nuts. This did, however, make me the best ever mother, granddaughter and daughter-in-law. I was so mellow they could have overthrown the government, and I would have said, "Good on ya, mate!" Instead I said, "Let's have pizza!" It was Mother's Day after all, who would deny me?

DAY 124

This is a story that you are not going to believe. But I swear to you it is absolutely true.

Do you remember my charming little red dress I purchased as a real boost? I couldn't wear it for Mother's Day dinner because it was unseasonably cold.

We all went to bed last night at a decent time and arose at different times like we all do. John and his mother, were both very early risers. John took the day off to golf and was going to leave later that morning. He would get the coffee started, read the paper, and quietly go about his business. Marie would go down in her housecoat, have her morning java, watch the birds and wait for John to finish the newspaper. If Rachel didn't stir, I would stay in bed until 7:30 or 8:00. On those days, Nana would usually beat me to the punch and get up, get dressed and have her coffee and share the paper.

Rachel was pretty tired from yesterday and was sleeping in. So I thought I'd do the same, especially since there were two other grown-ups in the house to watch Nana or help her out if need be.

I moseyed out of bed around eight. The smell of fresh-brewed coffee wafted up the stairs, and the group downstairs was chatting. It was right out of a Folger's commercial. I went to the bathroom, washed my face, brushed my teeth, but decided to leave my p.j.'s on since it was going to be a leisurely morning. As I descended the steps, I heard my husband say goodbye to the ladies and open the garage door.

The next sight I saw so horrified me that I screamed at the top of my lungs.

These were the words:

"Holy shit, just what the hell do you think you are doing?"

There sat Nana in my brand new, adorable, chic, I-was-going-to-be-the-toast-of-the-town dress. The white polka dots seemed to blink back at me as if to say:

"We have no idea what we are doing here, she took us hostage."

The bright red background sneered at me.

"See, everyone looks good in red."

I turned on the Benedict Arnold who sat next to her.

"Marie, she is wearing my brand new hundred dollar dress!"

"Well, I asked her where she was going all gussied up. I asked her if she had a boyfriend she was going to see."

The two of them laughed.

I was seeing stars or was it polka dots flying around the room. I was light-headed.

Then Nana did the unthinkable. She picked up her toast and began to reach towards her mouth. The strawberry jelly jiggled and swayed with her laughter. I saw the protoplasmic mass begin to slide from the crusted square towards that adorable white panel that demurely hid her 92-year-old cleavage.

"No!" I screamed and dove for the toast.

Luckily, she caught the dollop on her tongue before certain disaster.

"Get up those stairs and take that off. It's my hundred dollar dress, for God's sake."

I ran out to the car. I was incensed, enraged. I could not believe that my husband could yuck it up with these two insurgents before taking off for the golf course.

I caught him as he was driving away. I ran to the driver's side window. I banged on that window demanding recognition, retribution, remuneration anything that began with an "r."

"Didn't you see what Nana was wearing?"

"Yeah?"

He clearly had no idea what I was talking about. This was scary. He was getting used to me being crazy.

"It's my dress. My new dress. My hundred dollar dress."

Even I was beginning to realize this mantra is ridiculous.

"I thought she looked nice this morning."

"Uggh", I said quietly, "just go golfing."

"Sorry," he said. I know, however, that he had no idea what he was supposed to be sorry for. What was he supposed to do about Nana wearing this dress, which he didn't even know was my hundred dollar dress?

I stumbled back through the garage to the kitchen. Nana had come down in one of her own red dresses.

"Nana, what were you thinking?"

"Well, it was pretty and it was in my closet."

And so it was.

DAY 125

I put the dress in my own closet. Although to be honest, there was nothing the least bit childish or out of character for Nana to be opening her closet, rummaging through the contents, and choosing the most attractive new frock in the bunch. I knew I should have made her buy a new dress when we went shopping. She was so adamant that that pleasure was past her. She would have truly enjoyed a new dress. And now that I knew we wore the same size, much to my chagrin, I would take the next chance I got to go buy her her own new spring collection.

So even though for the last four months, Nana had proven to me time and time again that sometimes she was not capable of complete rational thinking, it occurred to me that she might not be the only one who lost her ability to think rationally. Sometimes, the problem was probably just living with a new person in the house. But add to that, the problem that I never knew when Nana would be completely rational or frustratingly childlike.... that's when I got caught. If I assumed that she was always to be treated like a child, she was very offended and rightfully so. So when she chastised me for such behavior, I reverted to my childhood.

"Nana, don't put those dishes in the sink, they can go in the dishwasher."

"Honey girl," she said, "I know that but there are only two or three dishes and I am perfectly capable of washing them, which is what I intend to do."

"Sorry," I would say apologizing like the day I got caught stealing pennies from the milk money.

Of course, on the other hand.

"Honey girl," she called down the stairs, "I don't have any clothes."

"Oh for Gods' sake, of course you do."

I went upstairs, and there was Nana in all her glory, not a stitch of clothing to be found anywhere. This was not a pretty sight, and I began laughing hysterically.

"Nana, what are you doing?"

"I was in my room looking through the things, and I don't have any clothes."

"Come with me," I said.

I walked her down the hall to her room.

"No, not this room, my room."

Why the cold wasn't bothering her now, I had no idea. But she continued to parade quite comfortably up and down the hallway like Gypsy Rose Lee.

She walked me back to my husband's office where there was a desk, a sofa bed and three filing cabinets all with the drawers open. Fortunately, my husband was not in there. This office was just a converted bedroom so there was a clothes closet along the back wall. To get to that closet, one needed to practically hike over a bevy of sales samples, folders of print information, some old video tapes and boxes of golf balls. Naked Nana figured out how to squeeze into the tiniest of spaces and slide open the closet door that revealed old Christmas boxes, winter coats, wedding gifts never opened and spare wallpaper from the baby's room.

"Nana, this is not your room; just come with me."

I unwedged her from the rock and a hard place she had put herself into and took her by the hand. We walked back down the hall to her room which is directly across the hall from the bathroom and next to the stairs.

"Why Nana naked, Mommy? We goin' swimmin'?"

"No, Rachey, Nana can't find her clothes."

"Okay," said Rachel.

And with that the toddler walked into Nana's room and opened a drawer at her height and pulled out some underpants and a bra.

"Here ya' go, Nana. Let's go watch Sesame Street!"

There would be no reason for Nana to wander down the hall "to her room." But there you have it. Lucid one moment, Lucy Ricardo the next.

You never really appreciate the finer points of clothing until you've had this experience.

DAY 130

"Hello?"

"Hi Cathy."

"Hi Mom."

I started to cry.

"Oh honey, what's the matter?"

"It's too hard, Mom. I don't know how you do this. It's just too hard. I want to kill both of them at alternate times during the day."

Mom was chuckling.

"MoMMM!"

"Sorry, honey. I understand; you know I do. It's just that you have two. Nana and I had six."

"But it's different. Nana isn't supposed to be like a child. She's supposed to be a grown-up."

"Cathy, this is the hard part. I know that. Do you really think that Nana and I never wanted to give up our day jobs with you kids? Nana is your mentor in many ways. You keep making the mistake of trying to get her to be that person all of the time. That's just not possible. This is what is so frustrating to all of us. We want Nana to be Nana—not part-time Nana and part-time baby, but that's the way it is. You have expectations for Rachel as well. Sometimes she comes through, and sometimes she doesn't. Like potty training—sometimes Rachel wants to be the big girl, and sometimes she really just wants to be the baby again. Nana's choices are often conscious maybe to get your attention or maybe to get what she wants."

"I am just so freaking tired."

"Honey, I'll be home in a month. You've done such a good job. Nana is doing just fine. And you know now how much your stepfather and I needed this break. I miss you very much, and it will be all over soon. I can't tell you how important this was to me, honey. I knew Nana would be safe and sound and not in some terrible nursing home with no love."

"I don't know how much love she feels like she's getting here. Even Rachel yells at her."

"It's okay, honey. Hang in there. I'll be home soon. I love you."

"I love you too, Mom."

After she hung up I said, "Hurry, please hurry."

I went and ate chocolate in the closet.

DAY 135

Spring had sprung. Nana was happy to be out in the sunshine and putter in the garden and throw the Frisbee to the dog. The dog was still frustrated that the Frisbee went nowhere. Troon actually had a very big soft spot for Nana. She thought I didn't know that she would sneak a snack to him more than occasionally. He probably gained ten pounds since she came here. He waited for her in the morning, and then he followed her around, just in case there was the potential for food. He would even play the dead Frisbee game because there was always a treat reward in the end. It was pretty remarkable how the dog helped the troop morale.

With the advent of warmer weather, Nana was looking for my wash line.

"Where do you hang the wash, honey girl?"

"I don't, Nana. I use the dryer."

"Well, that's a waste of electricity now isn't it?" she said accusingly.

"I don't have a wash line, Nana. And there's no place to put it. We live on a hill, and there's no even ground for a line."

"Honey, girl. You have five acres of ground here. You really can't find a place for a wash line?"

First of all, how did she know how many acres I had? Why is that bit of trivia stored in her memory banks? Second, I didn't want a wash line. I was lazy.

"Well, there's nothing I can do about it right now, Nana. So just put the clothes in the dryer, and we will deal with the wash line issue later."

"Harumph," she said.

But she had creative solutions to her problems. She draped her panties and bras on the deck chairs. She spread towels along the railing of the deck and covered the dry towels with her freshly washed and wet slips and shirts and dresses. Rachel was happy to see that Nana wore "big girl" panties too. Rachel had also noticed that Nana occasionally wore diapers. So she figured they were both in potty training. It gave her comfort to know she was not alone if there were an accident. So, in the spirit of sisterhood, I had to hang Rachel's "big girl" panties on the deck. Luckily, we live in the woods, so only the mailman and the UPS man were audience to this spectacle.

DAY 140

Cindy's cancer treatments continued. Nana and Rachel merely looked at this as another day out. In fact, the attention they garnered from the hospital staff, patients, families and volunteers, who surrounded the cancer unit, made them happy to be there.

I hated this job. I was not depressed by it. But it frustrated and angered me. We had been in and out of there so many times without any answers to our questions. The doctor would look at my sister, ask her the same inane questions, and we would come back for more.

The only important question, which is never answered is, "Why is this happening?"

Cindy was put on Tamoxifen as a study group. Initially, she was told she was not eligible for this drug because it was only for post-menopausal women. Pre-menopausal women did not have enough hormone receptors for the drug to be efficacious. How do you like that for medical speak? We all became experts under fire.

Cindy, however, was one of those beautiful aberrations who indeed had more than enough hormone receptors to be eligible for Tamoxifen. Of course, now the cancer had spread. So would it make any difference? Familiar words that you think you understand have new and not so sexy meanings in cancer therapy. "Cocktail" was now the mix of chemo for the day. "Tattoo" was what they did to you before they began your radiation treatment. Cindy thought she should have at least been able to get a heart, or a dolphin, instead of just a bunch of ugly blue moles around her chest.

Since today was a radiation day, it didn't have such a big downside. Cindy could probably have driven herself, which she often did (on morphine, if it's a bad day), but sometimes I think she just wanted the company. The company wasn't always a dream team either.

"Where are we going?" said Nana.

"To take Cindy to the hospital for radiation," I said as I strapped Rachel into her car seat.

"I don't want to go to the hospital."

"It's not for you, it's for Cindy."

"What's wrong with Cindy?"

"She has breast cancer."

"Didn't she have that taken care of?"

"Yes, Nana she did. But it came back and now she has to have radiation."

"I had radiation once."

"I know."

When Nana was 86 years old, somehow—I can't even begin to imagine how—they discovered that she had a vaginal cancer growth.

The treatment for this growth was to place her in a private room in the hospital. There she would be inserted with a radioactive tampon. Yes, I said a radioactive tampon. It would remain there for 24 hours. Then they would remove said tampon and give her a few weeks of radiation treatment.

My sister Caren and I went to visit her. But we were of child-bearing age and so, to protect us from the radiation, we had to remain in the hallway outside the door of Nana's room if we wanted to visit her. We could talk to her from the hallway, but we couldn't go into the room. So, in a hospital of sick people, we're trying not to shout too loudly to our 86-year-old grandmother.

"Hi, Nana, how are you?"

"What?"

"How are you feeling?"

"Well, a bit uncomfortable."

And then she would start laughing, and so would we. Hysterically. We were not well behaved.

When this debacle was over, Nana said this to me:

"Honey girl, how could I get sick down there? I haven't used that in years."

DAY 141

I'd discovered that Nana was a kleptomaniac. In my zeal to prepare Nana for her return to my mother, I started washing and packing up her winter clothes. I thought I would put them in her suitcase so that it wouldn't be too much packing when my mom came to pick her up. I took all the freshly laundered items up to her room and placed them on her bed. I went to the closet to retrieve the suitcase, and I found all manner of trinkets on the floor of the closet, on the shelf of the closet, and even clothing that didn't belong to Nana, neatly hanging *in* her closet.

On the floor were some of Rachel's toys. Now this I could easily have attributed to the two year old. Certainly, it would not be beneath Rachel to place her toys wherever she saw fit. But staring down from the top shelf were a stuffed reindeer, a decorative pillow from her crib and an E.T. doll, which nearly scared the crap out of me just like in the movie. There was no way on God's green earth my four-foot-high daughter put those things up there.

Being the Agatha Christie that I was, I also noticed my garden shoes on the floor of the closet, my mother-in-law's curlers that she kept here on the closet shelf, and a dictionary beside it. I could only conclude that Nana felt the need to play, garden and coif at emergency times when help was not available.

What the hell. I chuckled to myself, left everything where it was, took out the suitcase and gasped. It was filled, and I mean filled, with treasures from around the globe. I was stunned to see that she had successfully confiscated half my household without one ounce of suspicion from any of us. Never once had anyone said, "Have you seen my _____?"

There were bobby pins, shampoo, soap, Bounce, tissues, computer discs, photographs, candles, books, small statues, ribbon, gift bags, film canisters, stamps, envelopes, old magazines, aspirin, pens, tampons (I guess she liked that stay in the hospital), and various other things. Thank goodness none of it was perishable. The box of spaghetti was still intact.

I gave up. I left everything there and put her clean laundry in a big green trash bag and put it in the closet.

Three hours later, Nana dragged the big green trash bag down the stairs and said,

"What is this? This doesn't belong to me."

DAY 142

I couldn't decide which was worse, cancer or frustration. Of course, the obvious answer was cancer. That was a poem. "The obvious answer is cancer. But, is that easy when so much else makes you queasy?"

So you want to put cancer in that category of "well, at least nobody has cancer, so how bad could things be?" But when somebody does have cancer, then does it become the *only* thing that's bad? No. And that's bad. You still harbor grudges about the little things in life like why couldn't Nana behave herself when I had to take Cindy to chemotherapy? Not: "Why oh why did I have to take Cindy, my beautiful sister, only in her thirties, to chemotherapy?"

First, to concentrate on the horror of taking a 38-year-old to cancer treatment for basically three straight years crumbled me every day. So I would have to make each day more normal than the next when we were actually *in* the chemo stage. Second, Nana drove me goddamn crazy to shit.

So we were now back at the hospital. As usual, my sister was the one who was fine, accepting, and went along with the program with little or no complaints. Cindy parked herself in the big pink plastic chair with tubes of horrible, rancid crap running through her chest and into her veins, while she joked with the nurses.

They loved Cindy. Not like I did. I loved her like a sister. We loved each other because we have loved each other since we could see each other. We were not alike in every way. Besides being the pretty one, Cindy was always the bad one. I was the exemplary one. When I was afraid, she lived with abandon. Perhaps, she knew she had to for her time would be shortened. Even if she lived through all of this, spending her time in the correction of the cancer had limited her life choices. Cindy would never have willingly agreed to spend her time this way. It ruined the order of her life.

Besides being a rebel, she was also a Virgo and extremely organized. Normally, I would pooh-pooh this astrological hocus pocus, but my two sisters and my mother are all Virgos, and they are organized to a fault. They are neater than Felix Unger, and they each have the first dollar they ever earned. And the remaining two boys and two girls in my family would give Oscar Madison a run for his money, except we have no idea where our money is.

The nurses loved Cindy for her sense of humor. She was very funny. Her humor was usually self-directed and self-deprecating. She also remembered all of their children, their ailments and their complaints about their husbands. And she never, ever, ever complained to them about how much this sucked, how dreadful she felt when she went home, or how she never really wanted to see any of them again.

But our grandmother had to snit about every little thing.

"It's too cold in here."

"I know, Nana, that's why I brought you a sweater, please put it on."

"Well that baby of yours will catch her death of cold."

"I'm sure she won't, but notice if you will, that *she* is wearing her sweater like a good girl."

"You don't have to get testy about it."

Au contraire, I did have to get testy about it. I did not want to be here, not because it was inconvenient, or because my girls wouldn't behave, but because to be here was an admission. To be here was to give fact to the cancer. To be here meant she was dying, she was not living. I was angry. Perhaps that is what drove Nana's anger and bad behavior as well, but I did not give her credit for that. Only my anger and Cindy's, if she would show it, would be valid. Not that I was truly wishing Nana gone, but I wanted to be of service to our grandmother and my sister in the way that made sense in the cosmos. I felt like I was helping Nana live and Cindy die.

DAY 143

We were making plans to go on vacation. Cindy liked to go to my parents' exceedingly rustic cabin in Canada. There was no electricity, no running water, no traffic, no Nana. Okay, sue me. I just thought I'd tell the truth.

The charm of this barbaric experience was that you sort of pull all the required luxuries out of a hat, and if that didn't work, you didn't need or want it any way. For instance, although technically there was no running water, my stepfather—the prince of finagling—had created a system whereupon you started a gas-powered pump at the bottom of the hill where the spring pops up. You started the process much like you would a little gas lawn mower. You pulled the cord and hoped the engine started. If you were lucky enough to get that going (because you remembered to bring the gasoline, and you didn't have to drive twenty-five miles to go get it), you then connected the running pump to a hose that ran up to the cabin.

At the cabin, you took the pumping member of a hose up a six-foot ladder, as it throbbed in your hands. At the top of the ladder, you held the hose over two, fifty-five gallon drums and filled them with the freezing water that hovered in temperature around 10 degrees below zero which was cold enough to qualify as Canadian Spring Water. Of course, instead of bottling this ice cold dream stuff and making a fortune, we just bathed in it and froze our idiot American asses off.

When we just couldn't take it anymore, my stepfather developed an ingenious heating system. You would rise at the crack of dawn and light a fire under one of the drums. When the water was hot in the drum with the fire under it, you would fight to the death to be first in the shower because, as the hot water ran out, only a Mountie wanted that last shower.

We read by a gas light at night. We had big camp fires and roasted marshmallows. The mosquitoes loved them and us. We played killer pinochle. There was one big room upstairs and one downstairs. This cut down considerably on romance. Then again, all day fishing cuts down on romance, particularly if you were assigned filet duty. If you were lucky, you got lucky somewhere private during the Aurora Borealis. The mosquitos liked that too, as it brought out many a full moon, if you know what I mean.

In my world, this was extraordinary "roughing it." I think a Holiday Inn is roughing it. So to be considering this faux Canadian paradise for a vacation was not usually how I rolled. But at that moment in time, this was my idea of a vacation from the last six months, and I mean this sincerely when I tell you I could not wait to go. The mere act of planning this vacation for summertime put me in a better mood all day long.

DAY 145

The girls were back to their old tricks. It was as if the last six months never happened. I believed I was in the twilight zone of caregiving. I was downstairs vacuuming. I thought they were napping. They were cleaning the bathroom. Rachel was in the tub. Nana was back on her hands and knees scrubbing away. I peeked in. Déjà vu all over again. However, this time, there were no caustic substances in sight. Nana had an innocuous bucket of water, and Rachel was playing in a dry tub with a wash cloth and some toys. I snuck quietly back downstairs, had my ceremonial cup of coffee and then retrieved them just as they were finishing their self-assigned chores. I have no idea if either of them actually learned something from the previous bathtub fiasco, but it looked pretty damn harmless to me. Sometimes there is harmony in the world.

DAY 148

Against my better judgment, we were having a party. It was our 5th wedding anniversary and John's birthday. He was almost always opposed to a birthday party, but I read in a women's magazine somewhere that you should be ashamed of yourself if you don't celebrate the glory of your nuptials on a regular basis. It's a "who got you into this anyway?" kind of party. I didn't think that's what the magazine meant, but honesty was always the best policy.

These women's magazines had no basis in reality. I am firmly convinced that no woman with young children—job or no job—would create elegant centerpieces of carved squashes and radish roses, made from vegetables from her spring garden, for each table.

Bite that.

Which of course you could because these are vegetables right from your own spring garden.

Nevertheless, I wanted to have a party. I wanted to see my siblings and my friends, and secretly I wanted them to see the hell I'm in most of the time.

This would be a simple affair. I would make crock pot items like chili, hot dogs and sauerkraut and baked beans. I may have to offer Beano at the front door, but simplicity was the word of the day. There would be no decorations, and I would buy an ice cream cake from Dairy Queen to accompany the requisite "Happy Birthday" song for my husband's birthday portion of the celebration. Guests would be asked to bring chips, dip, potato salad and other sundry items. There would be free-flowing alcohol for all present. Each parent must watch their own children and could decide of their own accord whether said children were of drinking age or not. With the rules set down, and the head count recorded, we went to bed knowing the party would be a great success, or we would all be drunk and who cares.

DAY 150

A very nice party indeed. At least it began that way. Everyone was having a great time. We had beautiful weather. The kids played outside with the dog. John put up the volleyball net, and the parents and the childless had a great old time getting some fresh air and exercise. It was convivial. Let the games begin.

Yet, the men could not help themselves. As soon as a ball appeared, they all began acting like they were 10 or 11 years old. Did you ever notice how a game like volleyball brings out the barbarian in grown-up men? It's like the volleyball itself is imbued with testosterone, and each time they touch it, the response is more animalistic, more vicious and filled with aggression. There was no qualm about spiking a rock hard volleyball into the face of your sixty year old mother, if she was on the opposite team.

Because we had witnessed this on many occasions, the women conspired to refuse to play "girls against the boys." (An expression that used to make boys be nice to you and not try to give you a tonsillectomy with a ball). So we spaced the men between the women to tone down the vicious behavior.

I wish I could say this worked all the time. It worked for one or two games and then the testosterone ball started leaking into the women's bloodstream. I was not immune to this psychosis. My competitive spirit inhabited me like the headless horseman, and I grew as mad as if my pumpkin head was on fire.

"You cheated!" I yelled at my husband on our wood anniversary.

He and all his teammates laughed at me.

This was not good—for them.

"Fine," I bellowed.

"Fine," they all said mocking me.

I turned to the server, my younger sister "Kill them," I told her.

She nodded in agreement.

Her serve hit the net.

"Ha, ha, ha, ha," those lousy mockers replied.

She winked at me.

I winked back.

She blasted it over the net and onto the ground.

"Woooo!!!!" the women on our team screamed, "In your FACE!!"

I heard Rachel behind me.

"In your face too, Mommy."

I high fived her. This might not have been the right lesson.

Nana had been entertaining some of the little ones once the game began. So when I couldn't find Nana, I felt like less of a champion and more like a chump. I searched around the party guests, inside and out. I quietly ascended the stairs, wishing and hoping. The door to her bedroom was closed. Dare I open it?

I decided to check the bathroom first. On the floor in a trail to the toilet was a series of used and unused Depends. I quietly picked up the good, the bad and the ugly.

As soundlessly as I could, I went across the hall to Nana's bedroom and slowly turned the handle to peek into the room. There were dresses, stockings, hair ribbons and housecoats all along the bed railing like she had been trying to find the perfect outfit for the day's events. And Nana? She was fast asleep in her slip and stockings. I selfie high-fived and called it a good day.

DAY 151

I thought I'd take a different tack and let them decide what they would like to do to be entertained. Quite frankly, I was running out of ideas.

"Nana, what would you like to do today?" "I don't know, honey girl, what would you like to do?"

"I'd like to go to Paris, get a massage, walk on the Left Bank and drink wine in a café."

She laughed at me.

"I think I'd like to visit Mrs. Ginther."

"Okay," I said.

Nana was always quite well known in my town. Because she had worked at a few places downtown, had done all her shopping in the same town, and lived most of her life here, to be her granddaughter was quite the compliment. It was no small thing to go into any merchant in town and say, "I'm Margaret's granddaughter" and be treated with respect and dignity. And this was a big deal because in those days, and surely still today, teenagers were always seen as suspicious. If you weren't shopping with your parents or a grown-up, you were probably going to steal from the merchant. In every store we went into as teenagers, we were followed around either physically, or like those eyes-of-Jesus-pictures, someone was watching. So, I got to know many of Nana's friends and acquaintances as I grew up and grew older. And I was not above using my connections to "Margaret" to just be left alone to window shop.

Nana had a bevy of friends. They were very nice ladies. She had good friends and seemingly lots of laughs with them. But, as you can imagine, many of her friends were gone and long gone. As was dear, Bertha Ginther. The thing my sister and I loved about Bertha Ginther besides her jovial laugh, was her name. It was just fun to say "Bertha Ginther." When Nana said she wanted to visit Bertha, she really did know what visiting Bertha meant.

I took her to the cemetery. We parked the car and climbed out into the sunshine, warm breeze and scents of lilac. We gently wandered through the headstones, with Nana commenting on a friend here and an acquaintance there. We paused at our family plot with Pop-Pop, my dad, and some aunts and uncles. She bent over and pulled a few weeds. She whispered something in a sweet voice. Nana was in no hurry, not because of age, but because she was contemplative. We found Bertha. As she brushed back a lock of her hair, Nana gently touched the cold pink granite with dates of beginning and end. I became teary and left her to her moment.

I gave Rachel a tour of the cemetery, showing her angels and flags. Rachel ran around the monuments and picked dandelions and blew off their little, fluffy heads. There were balloons and flowers placed randomly around the headstones which made Rachel think this was some very quiet version of Chucky Cheese.

I saw Nana having some kind of a conversation or prayer over at Bertha's. She didn't seem sad. But this was hard for me. The forsythia was wildly in bloom, the grass was freshly cut. The birds were chirping happily in the trees. Rachel was doing the dance of Spring from grave to grave. I lingered for a time between the two of them. Gently, I called them both to the car and decided we all needed some ice cream.

DAY 152

We can't all be movie stars or race car drivers or the President of the United States. So to make the non-extraordinary bearable, we must engage in the ordinary in an extraordinary way.

My Nana was exemplary at this. She loved the beginning, middle and end of her day. When I was a child, and still to this day, she began her morning with the puzzles. Every day was a puzzle. We never knew what would happen. We might think it would just be an ordinary day, but there was bound to be an unexpected something or other that was not in the plan. So, she would start the day solving a few puzzles. That way she felt accomplished before the day even began.

I never remember Nana without a smile. Even at my house, she smiled every day. This must be the passage for the middle of her day. Habitual maneuvers were laid down more easily with a smile. Try it. Try to do the laundry, the cooking, the grocery shopping with a big fat smile on your face. You might look ridiculous; people might shy away from you in the produce aisle, but it makes it easier and far more pleasant. Often others will smile back, sometimes with that "I-have-no-idea-why-I'm-smiling-at-you" look. Who cares?

Nana still made the day's chores interesting and noteworthy. This commitment changed the ordinary to exemplary. Do your shoes shine like your mother made them shine when you were a kid? Are your whites as white as chalk because you didn't stop bleaching or scrubbing until they were perfect? Can you possibly fold T-shirts and towels as crisply as if they came from the Chinese laundry? These were the accomplishments of my matriarchs, because they refused to accept ordinary in any aspect of their ordinary work. I myself had not really latched onto this philosophy completely. I didn't do domestic routines with the vigor and exactitude imparted to me in my childhood. I would rather read a book and have slapdash t-shirts. Sometimes I would try, but honestly, put Nana's folding next to mine, and you would choose hers every time. So I think there was something zen about the way Nana and Mom did these things. Because they were both incredibly smart and interested and interesting. They did diligent work *and* read a book. I would search for the lesson here, because I knew there was one, but it might have meant admitting they did a better job than me. I would say that they both have taught me to do an excellent job where it matters, and I'd like to think that is what I do.

I tried to be as present in the day as Nana seemed to be. We picked our vegetables very carefully to make sure they were not bruised or would go bad too quickly. We actually lifted knick-knacks off the shelves and coffee table to dust under them, not just around them. Furniture polish was used for furniture, but Murphy's Oil Soap was for kitchen cabinets and hardwood floors Scouring pads were the correct tool for stainless steel but not Teflon. These were the important parts of working well in ordinary times. There was a twinkle in her eye when a job was well done.

At the end of the day, we would all usually settle down after dinner to watch television or read books. We took turns reading to Rachel. Sometimes it was during her bath, always when we put her to bed. Nana even rose to this task. I don't remember Nana ever reading bedtime stories to my brothers and sisters or to me. But somehow I can tell you Nana and my mother instilled a very deep love of reading into me. In every spare moment, they had a book in their hands. They barely watched TV, and neither of them watched it very much now. Their luxuries were well into the night. Long after the kids were in bed, the house was settled and quiet. Then between the pages of Leon Uris, Robert Ludlum, Richard Llewellyn; this is where they took off into extraordinary worlds, not to escape their own, but to view the trials and tribulations of others so that they knew the joy of ordinariness.

Sometimes I pray at night that the Lord will give me the beauty of another ordinary day, because I know that no one gets through life unscathed, and that I will be in a day where I will pray for ordinariness to return in all its peace and glory, hopefully with a big ass smile on my face.

DAY 154

How to make life interesting for all of us on a rainy day? Even a sunny day for that matter. I had exhausted McDonald's (for Rachel), laundry (for myself) and anything after 7A.M. (for Nana). I needed a muse, a sign, a Broadway show with Barney and Ruby Keeler and Frank Zappa. Was there such a thing?

I decided to get in the car and start driving. Maybe we would take a tour of nursing homes. Oh how ugly was that! Okay, then daycare centers. But then that left me with Nana, and she was not my first choice. It's not what you think. It's just that she didn't nap, and she was onto me most of the time. So I couldn't fool her as easily.

We played at the park for fifteen minutes, and that ran its course. I caved in, and we returned to the land of chicken nuggets and French fries. We had now used up forty-five minutes.

Somehow I knew I would want this precious forty-five minutes back again someday, but right now it was like a tapeworm I just wanted to feed it enough so it would go away. But if you feed a tapeworm, it would just come back for more.

I had this brilliant idea. Okay, it was Rachel's idea.

"Zoo, mommy."

"No zoo, honey, too far away, and Nana can't walk that much."

"Yes, I can," said the 92 year-old.

I honestly thought, "What the fuck?"

"Okay," I said, "the zoo it is."

The zoo was a thirty-minute drive. If you felt like making a donation, it cost one dollar to enter. I paid five dollars for the privilege of challenging a 92-year-old to prove herself a worthy adversary.

I am repaid a thousandfold.

We saw the monkeys just as we entered. Excitedly, Rachel jumped in unison with them. She squealed; they squealed. She laughed; they laughed.

Nana wandered over to the duck pond. Rachel followed.

"Feed the duckies, Mommy, pleaaaaaases?" she whined before I could even say no.

"Give her a quarter, honey girl," Nana chimed in.

Why would I argue? This would keep them occupied, but I can't help myself.

"No," I said.

Why do parents always say no before they say yes? This was a learned response. There was no way on God's green earth that a toddler could possibly ask for something reasonable. Unless it was to go to the bathroom during potty training which never happened. Therefore, "no" was always the first correct answer. I suspected this was true with teenagers as well. Even though I didn't have one, I was one, and I am certain that a negative response to any request would have been absolutely appropriate.

Nana fished a quarter out of her ever-present handbag and handed it to Rachel's fat little outstretched fingers. They communicated without me, beyond me. Flabbergasted, I watched the transaction.

Rachel, two-year-old Rachel, went to the duckie food dispenser, put in her quarter, ever so slowly manipulated the knob and tried to catch the kibble with her hand. Most of it ended up on the ground.

"Mooooommmmyy, I drop it," she cried, her little heart broken.

"Now look what you've done," Nana retorted to me with the evil eye.

"I _____?" I was speechless.

I hugged her hard and wiped her tears.

"It's okay honey, take what you have and feed it to the ducks, and Mommy will get you some more."

She sniffled back the insult of the machine and ran to the lake to toss little chunks directly into the faces of the ducks. They were not unsuspecting. They awaited her arrival like kitchen staff that was abominably late. I was certain the ducks had mastered the sound of the turning knob.

I put three quarters in the machine, and we spent the next half-hour feeding the ducks that probably should have been on Jenny Craig the way people haphazardly threw food at them.

Nana moved gingerly to a nearby bench and sat patiently while Rachel fed those ducks with gusto. We strolled around for fifteen more minutes. We watched the bobcat, the bison, the cows and the pigs. It was a very eclectic zoo.

"Mommy, I tired."

"Me, too," said Nana.

I thought, "I win!" but in my heart I knew they won again. They always won. I had a learning disability when it came to them.

DAY 155

I tried to keep my husband out of this. He was usually not around when the sky was falling anyway. That is not to say that he was not helpful—to the contrary. It was just that the girls seemed a bit more behaved when he was around. It's like you're born with this innate sense that you better straighten up and fly right when Daddy gets home. Even Nana. The minute John walked in the door, most of her senses reappeared with amazing alacrity and clarity.

Nana wouldn't dream of walking around without her teeth, her hair ribbon or her clothes for that matter, if she knew John was around. Now that I think about it, she was much more sensible on the weekends than during the week. Rachel would roll with the tide, if the tide was full on Wednesday and ebbed on Friday night through Sunday night—that was fine with her.

The upshot of this was:

No one believed me.

I sounded like a raving maniac.

My job looked easy when people were watching.

I imagined this is what a professional golfer or tennis player feels like.

"Gee," everyone thinks, "I could do that."

"It doesn't look THAT hard," one might say to herself as Tiger chips one in from 120 yards over a sand trap and a water hazard with the wind blowing forty miles per hour in his face.

I resented this. Like Tiger and Serena and Venus, I practiced every day to be a good mother and a good caregiver. I worked very hard to keep my patience, keep the troops entertained, made sure they were well-fed, bathed when necessary, their teeth brushed and their hair combed. I was diligent about keeping them presentable to society, watching their manners, their bowel movements and their antics.

But today's purpose was to examine the behavior of Nana and Rachel in the face of Dad.

Dad would wake up early, make the coffee and putter around the house on a Sunday morning. When Rachel would wake up, I would leisurely get out of bed. Without fail, Rachel would call me from her bed.

"Mommy, come get me."

"Rachey, you can get out of bed yourself."

"No, I want you to come."

"Why don't you come here to Mommy's room and we can snuggle in Mommy's bed for a little while?"

"No, come get me in my bed, Mommy."

So, I put on my robe over my ratty, holey t-shirt and shuffled off to her bed. I stood in the doorway, with my eyes trying to focus.

"Okay, I'm here."

"No, come here and get me."

"Oh for heaven's sake, Rachel, just get out of bed."

She just looked at me.

I went to her bed. Give her a big hug and a tickle.

"Okay honey, Mommy's here. Let's go see what Daddy's doing."

"Yay, Daddy!"

And with that, she jumped out of bed and bounded down the stairs as fast as possible. Meanwhile, back at the kitchen, Nana was deep in her coffee and newspaper by now. She had not spilled anything, started any fires or caused any trouble whatsoever. How did I know this? John was home.

"Good morning, Nana," I said.

"Good morning honey girl," she responded brightly.

"Hiya' Nana!" yelled Rachel. Sometimes Nana heard and sometimes she didn't, so Rachel didn't take any chances any more. I think she would have slapped Nana heartily on the back to greet her partner if she could have reached Nana's back.

"Well hello there, sweetie, would you like some toast and cocoa?"

"Yes, please," bellowed Rachel politely.

Who are these people?

Daddy entered on cue. Did they practice this little morality play while I was vacuuming, paying bills, taking a shower?

"Hello, my beauties," he said ever so sweetly.

Rachel and Nana giggled flirtatiously.

I rubbed my temples in wonder. I blinked my eyes a few times, trying to focus on this Father Knows Best scenario.

"Uh, hello? What's going on here?" I asked.

They all looked at me accusingly. I knew it. It was a conspiracy. They have cooked this little thing up between them to make me look bad in front of the boss. Oh, how stereotypes die hard. The working man was the boss, and the rest of us are lucky to be the peon.

"What?" I said.

"Mommy cranky," said Rachel.

"Mommy is NOT cranky. Mommy just wants to know why you two are so much better behaved when Daddy's home," I sniffled. I figure if I pretended my feelings were hurt, it would add credibility to my argument.

"Daddy not cranky," she said.

"Well, of course not. He's the one who gets all the good behavior. He's the one who sees shining, happy faces. Daddy never sees cranky Rachel or cranky Nana. Noooooo. Daddy only sees that Mommy must be out of her mind because you two are helpful, kind and brave like a bunch of boy scouts," I retorted. I was retorting to a toddler.

"Honey girl?" asked Nana without looking up from her newspaper, "could you make some more coffee?"

We all pretended this never happened.

"Of course," I said with a light airy voice, "that's what I was just about to do."

DAY 160

We are getting close to the end. On the face of it, it doesn't look like we've had much progression. It's not like a love story where you wait to see if she gets the guy. It's just a life story, not much happens, but what does happen, happens to everyone. And, as Willy Loman's wife says "Attention must be paid."

This was where the nursing home conversation got tricky. Not one of us wanted to even consider such a thing. Nana was as healthy as a horse, but we just didn't know if she could sustain her ability to care for herself.

My stepfather believed that he had already given over more than he should have. My grandmother had lived with them in three different places. First, they put her upstairs in her own apartment. Then, when the fourteen steps inside and twenty-two steps outside seemed to be a bit much for an 85-year-old lady, my stepfather relented and built a small apartment in the back of the house. One large room semi-divided by walls with a diminutive kitchen, bath and bedroom big enough for a single bed. A sweet living room with a big bay window overlooking the woods gave Nana lots of privacy and nature.

Eventually, she had to come into the house when the kids left and take one of their rooms, so that the apartment could be rented for extra income.

Now mind you, Nana had lived in her own home for twenty years when my mother came home husbandless and moved in. Years later, my mother bought that home from Nana as a protection for her future. Then Mom got married, and my stepfather decided that home could be rented as a source of income, and Nana should move in with us. I will be forever grateful for that boorish decision because Nana was always there when we were having our teen angst and traumas—half of which were caused by my stepfather.

Even though a nursing home would be the last straw, I was expected to report on Nana's behavior to gauge the possible timing for such a decision. I refused. I did want to rant to anyone who would listen to how crazy my days and nights were, I would not be party to the "N" decision to make life easier on anyone.

Who made life easier for Nana—ever? No one. What we were doing for her was a pittance. So I learned that when my Mom called, I needed to maintain an air of dignity and calm, in the face of the typhoon that surrounded me.

When Mom called today to say that she would be home in three weeks, I tried not to sound like Jesus Christ was finally arriving. Just before the phone rang, I was putting Rachel on the potty while Nana sat down to count her money. She loved her money. She had to count it, look at it, and hold it most of the day. She never let go of the whereabouts of her purse. She brought it down in the morning and took it up to bed with her at night. Even if we weren't going anywhere, that purse stayed in its assigned location and was only moved at the scheduled time.

"Pooh, pooh potty, Mommy," Rachel said.

"Good girl!" I exclaimed, this advice from friends and relations to make potty training the rapture of our lives.

The phone jangled.

"Nana, can you get that?"

Yes, I would still let her answer the phone. It gave her props, and I couldn't always run to the phone. What she did with the phone when I wasn't paying attention, who knew, but I didn't care.

"Hello? Yes. Why don't you talk to her? Honey girl, it's for you."

Of course it was for me. Who would it be for? Rachel didn't know her phone number yet.

"Hello?"

"Hi, honey, it's Mom. I don't know why she won't talk to me. Is she still mad at me?"

"Wait, I'll ask. Nana, are you mad at Mom?"

"What?"

"Are you mad at Mom?"

"Oh honey girl, my mother's been gone a very long time; of course I'm not mad at her."

"Did you hear that?" I ask my mother.

"Yes, well that's good I guess."

"Mom, she's fine. She doesn't hear all that well when she doesn't want to, and she probably didn't realize it was you."

"Well, how are you?"

"I'm fine. We're trying to potty train. So accidents abound."

"Can I talk to Rachel?"

"Sure."

I took the phone into the bathroom where Rachel is reading a Good Housekeeping magazine.

"I reading, Mommy."

"Good girl, Nanny wants to talk to you."

I hand her the phone.

"Hiya' Nanny."

I can't hear the other end of the conversation but the gist is clear.

"I poopin' on the potty."

"Yes."

"Yes."

"Bye."

As Rachel handed me the phone, I heard my mother's voice trail off in the distance:

"...and you be a good girl for your mommy, okay?"

"She handed the phone back to me, Mom."

"Oh, okay."

"So what's happening?"

"Nothing really, we wake up, we do breakfast, we do errands, we do lunch, we do nap, we do dinner, we do bedtime. It's pretty basic," I said.

"It's not *that* easy," she said.

"Mom, Nana's fine, we are doing well really. I can't wait to see you. But Nana's really comfortable here. Rachel and Nana are like sisters now, and it's really okay."

"Okay, then," she said with a hint of doubt in her voice, "I'll talk to you soon. I love you."

"I love you too. Bye."

The two girls were reading in the bathroom. Rachel was still on the potty, and Nana was sitting on the step stool I had there for Rachel to wash her hands.

"...If you really want whiter whites the only solution is a bleach solution."

"I like beach," said Rachel.

"That's right, honey, Nana likes bleach too because it gets our messy panties as white as white can be."

"Mommy, get baiting suit, Nana and me go to da beach."

There were never such devoted sisters.

DAY 170

Ten days to go. I could feel that Nana sensed something. I was doing laundry like a madwoman. I was cleaning up and out and over everything. Partly because my mom was a clean freak, and partly to get all of Nana's things together in preparation for her leaving.

"What are you doing?" said Nana, as she observed me going through her closet, her drawers, under her bed, in her bed. I was the huntress. I would not stop until I had every single stitch of clothing that she brought with her cleaned, folded and smelling April fresh for her return to my mother's.

"I am looking for your dirty clothes," I said with my head wedged between the bed and the wall.

"What?"

I swear to God, if I could I would remove *what* from the dictionary. Anyone found saying "What" in my kingdom would be tarred and feathered. No questions asked.

"Honey girl, my dirty clothes are in the hamper," the vixen said with her innocent smile.

"Not all of them," I burst out victorious as I waved an enormous pair of underpants in the air like an Olympic flag carrier.

"Those aren't mine," said Nana.

Do I take the bait or do I let it go? Ten more days. What did it matter whose underpants they were? Maybe she was sleeping with the Jolly Green Giant after I went to bed. Maybe Rachel had a secret supply of large-and-in-charge undergarments. Maybe my husband was wearing ladies' underwear, and I'm going to be on Jerry Springer in the very near future.

I gritted my teeth.

"Okay," I said, "but whoever owns them has to have them washed."

"Why are you washing only my things?"

"Um, uh, because I think I'm running out of hot water, and I want you to be the first to have all her wash done." Oh Lord, I prayed, please do not strike me dead.

"Oh, honey girl, that will never do. You have to do the man's wash first. After all he's a working man and needs his things when he needs them."

My voice rose a bit too much.

"Don't you worry about my man. I take care of him just fine. Now get your stuff out of the hamper, so we can wash it and pack it."

Oh crap.

"What?"

Thank God for "What."

"I said, we need to wash it and stack it so we can put it away neatly for another day."

"Okay, honey girl, but I will do the folding and stacking; you're just not very good at it yet."

DAY 171

I smelled freedom. This was an evil and vile thing I was thinking. Do you know how long it took my grandmother to smell freedom? Never. When she came to live with me, she was dependent upon my mother and my stepfather. Before that, she lived with one of us six children until they moved her out of her house. A house that she bought under the nose of her drunken husband so that she could have a home of her own. When she moved out of her beloved Hanover Street, my sister Cindy was living there with her husband, toddler son, and my youngest brother, a high school kid who could no longer tolerate the antics of my stepfather.

Perhaps, Nana never really wanted the freedom I crave. Perhaps I'm full of shit. I feel quite certain that Nana, a woman of great intellect, enormous heart and wisdom would have relished a moment or two to think. Often during these last ten years or so, I would find Nana lying across her bed, feet dangling off one side with her hand over her eyes, her glasses carefully placed on the bedside table. I always assumed she was taking a nap. Now I think otherwise; she was very likely shutting out the world for just a brief moment so that she could compose her thoughts, her insight for the next needy soul who walked through her door. There was never enough time for contemplation. This was done with the crosswords, the cryptoquote, church. Those were the places where she could turn her thoughts any which way and mold and shape her influence. I don't think she thought of it this way, I just think that's what was happening. She had to be too damn tired at the end of the day—what with perfect t-shirts to fold and bathrooms to clean—to give even a brief second to contemplation.

I don't even know what my brand of freedom was going to look like. I just believed that some great pressure would be released if I could just be a toddler's mom and not a nonagenarian's mom. Freedom's a funny thing. With privilege comes responsibility. Freedom is what got me into this mess, since no one thought I was doing much anyway. Of course, that's how I came to be with Nana. As I was wiping down the kitchen counter thinking all these thoughts, it occurred to me that Nana found freedom within.

DAY 172

Up to this point I have avoided all talk of sex. This was for many reasons. First, my husband would kill me. This was a very private man which is one of the reasons he didn't appear in many of these pages. Of course, most of the time he was on the road and not around, so his appearance would have been fictitious. But he did appear on occasion at home, and when he did, it was often in the role of one who was befuddled about the expectations that go along with being a father and a grandson-in-law. This was not because he was without intelligence or capabilities. John was a highly respected and brilliant salesman and manager. But none of those skills carried any weight around here. Just ask me. I was still trying to figure out how thirty-thousand- dollars-worth of education had prepared me for the last six months of refereeing, herding, watching, listening, and keeping the peace. Perhaps international relations would have been a better course of study, but alas, that ship had sailed. I could only yell "objection" so many times, in the hopes that one or the other around here would stop what they were doing and heed my warning.

Nevertheless (a legal term, so as not to lose what valuable tactics I had learned so far), my husband and I had seen a serious downturn in our intimate moments. Even an occasional peck between the two of us rendered Rachel into serious giggles, or the word "yuck" was heard for the next twenty minutes as she wandered around the house.

"Yuck, Barney, Mommy and Daddy kissin'."

"Yuck, yuck, yucky, Nana," she exclaimed as she drove out of sight on her plastic horsey.

"Fine!" I said.

It was bad enough this two year old had anything to say about her parents, let alone her parents' PDA (public display of affection—I heard it on The Real World while I was sneaking a look at MTV). But then the grandmother would render an opinion.

"You kids need to get a room," she would say if she saw my husband love tap me on the fanny.

So affection, caring, cuddling, touching, anything like that would breed contempt around here. We had given in insofar as we were willing to leave slap-and-tickle in the bedroom. But there was no time for such games when the world around us never slept, or wandered, or wanted to climb in bed with us.

We would wait as long as we could for the persons in the house to breathe soundlessly through the baby monitor. And one of two things would happen. It would be us who were breathing soundlessly and out cold, or with the first sign of affection, a door handle would turn. One of us would jump up, run for the door to see who was wandering, and if it didn't take too long, hope for the best in a few minutes.

One lazy wintry Sunday, we decided to devilishly try an amorous encounter during naptime. I heard weird noises coming out of the bathroom in the hallway at the most inopportune moment, and let it be. Upon investigation a while later, when the culprit had returned to her room, I found My Pretty Little Pony taking a shower. I have no idea who the culprit was, but I was relaxed enough not to care.

So my husband and I devised a particularly ingenious plot to keep the yucksters at bay. The plot was only good under extremely specific circumstances, but nonetheless necessity had become the mother of invention. We decided that we must outwit these two by getting them to bed early. This involved such things as intense physical activity and/or a large, tryptophan-laden meal as a late dinner, which would send them scurrying off to bed.

We decided to use the DOUBLE whammy of lots of activity and a turkey dinner. We took Nana and Rachel to the Please Touch Museum and enjoyed a lovely turkey dinner when we get home. All was well in tryptophan heaven.

DAY 173

At my regular brunch, my girlfriends were discussing their parents as I was discussing Nana. We realized that we were not honoring the elderly. Sally's mother recently passed away, and she was sharing the experience with us. Luckily, it was brief and not too traumatic. Her mother was 90 and had a severe stroke, went into a coma and died forty-eight hours later without regaining consciousness. My mother said, "We should all be so lucky." She was right, of course, and although it sounded coarse, my mother was speaking from a vantage point of one who was closer to old age if not death (or so we think, but who ever knows?), and has a mother who is in her nineties.

But we spoke of how we eventually come to honor our elderly when it is too late. I admitted that I rarely took the time to take advantage of Nana's wisdom, understanding, counsel, fortitude, knowledge, piety and fear of the Lord (the seven gifts of the Holy Spirit for those of you who were raised Catholic). But it was still in there. Those gifts Nana shared with me when I was so young, were still a part of her. Admittedly, they were hard to find most of the time, but I wasn't even looking.

We took our own four-person poll and tried to come up with a recipe we could use in the future. We also thought we might need to pass this on to our sons and daughters, even granddaughters.

Listen to your elders. Not in the sense of paying attention, but in the sense of really listening. We had all experienced that sometimes you'll have no idea what your mother or grandmother is talking about, and other times you will find pearls of wisdom beyond your ken. For instance, I remembered when Nana's parting advice when I went to college was, "a stiff prick knows no conscience." It seemed crude at the time, but it means so many things about men and their world.

Try to maintain their dignity even while they are incapable of such behavior. Terri's father-in-law once took his teeth and dropped them on the floor in the middle of a restaurant. This seemed like no big deal in the scheme of things, but your inclination is to scold your elderly parent into behaving more appropriately. Nothing could be further from the truth. Even scolding your children only works half the time. Terri was much better at maintaining her dignity and that of her father-in-law. She just used her napkin to gingerly pick up the teeth and placed the napkin unobtrusively on his bread plate. This would have worked fine except the waiter grabbed the bread plate and the teeth went flying across the room. But that was not Terri's fault. Now, the waiter had to come up with a dignified response for *his* beastly behavior.

Take some time with those who are old. Don't just pick them up and take them out for a meal with a bunch of other people. Take them out by yourself. They will feel special and know that you are interested in them. Call them and ask about their day, their meals, the neighbor's dog. None of this will interest you, but you will be honoring them by acknowledging their existence. It is not easy, but rest assured when your mother, father, grandparent is gone, you will know that you gave them credence. I told the girls about how my mother just wanted to get Nana out and about one fine autumn day. The entire car ride was a constant "Oh my, how beautiful!" and "Aaahhh that's lovely" when surrounded by the reds and golds and oranges of maples and oaks and sassafras. Mom found herself enjoying the ride as much as Nana.

Ask them about their lives in the past. First of all, this is where their best material lies. They remember details from 1943 with more clarity than you can remember what you had for lunch yesterday. This is where you will find your treasure trove. Their lives were fascinating. They lived through two World Wars, a Depression, the birth of the airplane, television, the first man on the moon, and the arrival of computers in every house. Our life pales in comparison to the things they have seen and actually lived through. It is not boring, trust me. I loved when Nana would regale me with tales about her work during WWII, how she kept her family fed during the Depression, and why she had no use for microwaves (the food doesn't taste as good--take time cooking it tastes better, she said. And BTW she was right about that.)

Brush their hair. If they have no hair, polish their shoes. Do something "intimate" for your elder, and you will be connected to them like you haven't been since they held you in their lap. Even mothers and fathers lose intimacy with their children when they no longer bathe them, cut their bangs, tie their shoes or zipper up their coat. These small chores connect you to their hands, their eyes, their hearts. And you usually end up touching them in some way. Elder people have lost the fine art of touch. We all know that babies who are not touched fail to thrive and die—we all need that—even our Grandmas and Grandpas. So find a small intimate chore you can assist with such as helping them button a coat, fix a hat, tie a tie…something…anything to connect.

My girlfriends and I think that we will all benefit from looking a little closer at the people who brought us into and up in this world. Anonymity among loved ones is a blight not a blessing.

DAY 180

Nana has left the building. She went home two days ago. First, I breathed a huge sigh of relief. That actually lasted two days. I finally came down off that feeling and started to experience empty nest syndrome. I spent every waking and sleeping hour of the last six months wondering where Nana was, what damage she was causing, what kind of trouble she was getting into and how would that involve Rachel? I was having the hardest time "turning that off." Rachel would be in the family room watching a video and singing along, and I panicked because I couldn't see or hear Nana. I let the dog out for a few minutes, and I would see him wandering up and down the driveway and Nana was nowhere to be found. I ran outside and called her, and then I realized that she was at my mother's house.

Sometimes, I felt bad about this, as if I were shirking a great duty, like I sent my child out for adoption. Other times, I was so relieved that even the guilt that washed over me couldn't scrub away the smile on my face. It's ugly to be Catholic and guilty. An old Jewish boss of mine once said the Jews and Catholics could share the same church—Our Lady of Perpetual Guilt.

Rachel and I seemed to be getting along a bit better these days with just us. We were more carefree. We could come and go with more speed and less worry about moving at a snail's pace. But Rachel missed Nana too even though she didn't know how to express this.

"Mommy, no nap today," she would say.

"Oh, I don't think so," I would tell her, "you are so tired, and you can't even keep your eyes open."

"Nana doesn't want a nap, either," she said.

"How do you know that?" I asked her.

"She told me," she would reply innocently.

"How could she tell you that, Rachey, Nana is at Nanny's house?"

"No, Nana upstairs," Rachel said.

"Honey, you know Nana went home. She's not here anymore," I told her.

Rachel started to cry hard with real tears.

"I want Nana; she helps me," she sobbed.

"I know honey, she helped me too; I just didn't know it at the time."

I put Rachel to bed, and although she cried for a few minutes, she went to sleep quickly.

I started some housewifely chores like laundry and vacuuming and that lasted about two minutes before I pick up the phone.

"Hi Mom? How's Nana?" I asked her.

"She's fine, dear. Why do you ask?"

"Oh, Rachel misses her a bit. How about you? How are you adjusting?"

"Oh, it's okay. Your stepfather and grandmother are fighting over important things like how to fill the sugar bowl and who should go get the mail in the afternoon."

"I know it's hard, Mom." I told her sympathetically, as it all came rushing back to me. "I could take her for a day or two when you need a break," I told my mother.

"No, honey. I don't think that would work. You know how much she hated coming to your house and then how hard it was for her to come back here after getting settled in with you. She and I have lived together for a long time. We'll be fine. But you could come take her out for lunch with Rachel or just for a drive to the mall. That way I could keep a little peace around here and maybe get a few things done."

"That would be fine, Mom. I'm not sure about the mall. Nana is just a little too comfortable there, if you remember."

We both laughed. It's not a hearty laugh. We wished we didn't have to talk about Nana this way. It's like she was a commodity and not a person. And not a good commodity all the time at that.

"Besides," my Mom said, "you need to rest, because there's always next year."

NEXT YEAR

Although technically it was next year, it was really only a little over six months since Nana left. Now the two partners in crime were three and 93. It had to be better this time, right? Rachel had been anticipating Nana's arrival since Christmas. Once all the toys, decorations and Santa threats were put away for the season, Rachel immediately turned to the next exciting thing to happen. "Nana is coming!"

"Mommy?" she asked me over breakfast one day.

"Yes, Rachel," I responded.

"How soon will Nana be here?"

"Why, honey?"

"'Cause I need to get ready."

"What do you have to do to get ready?"

"I have to give her some of my toys; and I have to make her bed with a special blankey; and I have to say bye-bye to Nanny."

"Why do you have to give Nana some of your toys?"

"I don't know why, Mommy, but Nana never brings any of her own toys to our house. And she probly needs some to play with while I'm sleeping or at school. Plus Nana shouldn't play with Troonie's toys anymore 'cause he has icky dog breath."

I could barely keep a straight face.

"Why do you have to say bye-bye to Nanny?"

"Oh Mommy, did you forget that's why Nana comes here. Nanny has to leave her here, so we can babysit while Nan goes to Farida."

"Oh yeah, thanks for reminding me."

So Nana was coming again. Rachel picked out some toys that she didn't like or didn't play with anymore and put them in Nana's room. She had picked out a nice set of sheets and a fresh comforter for Nana's bed. And she brought an important addition to Nana's room.

"Here Mommy, Nana needs this," she said as she walked in with her old baby monitor that I had placed in the back of her closet.

"What does Nana need that for?" I asked her.

"In case she's cryin' and you can't hear her. I don't want to have to get up and help her, Mommy. That's why Nanny is making *you* babysit."

About the Author:

Cathy Sikorski has been a significant caregiver for the last 25 years for seven different family members and friends. A published humorist, Sikorski is also a practicing attorney who limits her practice to Elder Law issues. Her combined legal and humor expertise has made her a sought after speaker where she tackles the Comedy of Caregiving and the legal issues that affect those who will one day be or need a caregiver (which is everyone).

Along with her speaking engagements, Sikorski is a frequent guest on radio programs and podcasts where she talks about the importance of using humor in caregiving. With more than 30 years of law behind her, she provides critical legal information for our aging population. Her latest endeavor is her humorous memoir *Showering with Nana: Confessions of a Serial (killer) Caregiver (HumorOutcasts Press 2015)*. Sikorski has participated in memoir writing classes for two years at the prestigious Fine Arts Work Center in Provincetown, Massachusetts. She has also participated in the Philadelphia Writer's Conference where she won a Humor Prize in 2014. Sikorski writes for *The Huffington Post* and is a contributing author for the HumorOutcasts.com and she can been seen on the West Chester Story Slam YouTube channel. Known as a "Thought Leader," her work can be found in the *HappinessRecipe Anthology: The Best of Year One*, published 2014. Sikorski maintains an active blog "You just have to Laugh…where Caregiving is Comedy…" at www.cathysikorski.com where she continues to post absurd yet true stories that continue today.

You can contact Cathy Sikorski at cathy.sikorski@gmail.com and follow her on Twitter at @cathy_sikorski.